VISIONARY LEADERSHIP

A STUDY IN LEADERSHIP DEVELOPMENT

Pastor Ronnie,
Few are both shepherd
and leaders... you are.
May God surround you with
men and women hungry to serve.

[signature] Ph.D.
III John 2

BY

STAN E. DEKOVEN, PH.D.

VISIONARY LEADERSHIP

A STUDY IN LEADERSHIP DEVELOPMENT

PUBLISHED BY:

VISION PUBLISHING, 1115 D Street

RAMONA, CA 92065

WWW.VISIONPUBLISHINGSERVICES.COM

1-800-9-VISION

ALL SCRIPTURE REFERENCES ARE TAKEN FROM THE KING JAMES VERSION, NEW INTERNATIONAL VERSION AND NEW AMERICAN STANDARD VERSION OF THE BIBLE UNLESS OTHERWISE NOTED.

PRINTED IN THE UNITED STATES OF AMERICA

PREFACE

The lack of lay leadership to carry out the biblical mission of the Church is a major problem in Christianity. A key factor in this is the failure to understand and teach others some of the basic "how to" aspects of Christian leadership.

The Word of God is filled with examples of people who were leaders, whether they had great gifts and abilities or were weak and despised. However, all of the men and women the Lord used then, as well as now, had to develop their skills by study and practice. Charisma may inspire, but true leaders are made, trained and function well or poorly because of that training.

This book is designed to be a practical help for those resolved to make the most of the time they have, and to become the leaders that God would use for His Kingdom. It is not filled with theory, but has its foundation in God's Word to prepare and encourage the growth of leaders for our desperate times.

THE CITY

Since the turn of the century, there has been a global, massive move of the population from rural to urban centers. The vast majority of people are now living in major cities, many with tremendous challenges that the Church has been ill equipped to face.

The focus of this movement is to challenge and equip men and women who will have a heart for leadership where the people need it most. We need leadership in suburbia, but the most outstanding opportunities lie in the urban centers of the developing nations and the third-world.

My hope is that man will hear the cry of the city, and develop a "*Vision for their community,*" and consider taking a place of leadership where maximum impact can occur. For those that do, challenge will certainly await them. But, with every challenge, if we are humbly submitted to the Lord, He will empower us to go beyond our natural capabilities and enjoy the fruit of spiritual leadership. Souls will be saved, men and women discipled, missions fulfilled, and God's Kingdom will be extended.

PREFACE to SECOND EDITION

FOLLOW ME!

At 23 years of age I joined the Army. The circumstance surrounding my enlistment is not germane, but my experience, especially in Officer Candidate School was a life changer. Through the highly structured, disciplined and stressful process of military training, I learned more about leadership than I could have from a thousand books. I learned to lead by following the leader.

One thing that struck me when I first arrived at Fort Benning, Georgia, home of the U.S. Infantry, was the statue found in front of the post. Depicted is a soldier with a bayonet thrusting forward an arm overhead, and a caption underneath says, "Follow me!"

Leadership requires someone to be out front, to take the helm, to give direction, to take a risk, to risk defeat. No wonder good leaders are hard to find. But, good leaders must be found, molded, shaped and encouraged to be like the soldier at Ft. Benning willing to stand up as Paul of old and boldly declare, **"Follow me!...as I follow Christ!"**

ACKNOWLEDGMENTS

So many people are contributors to any work. There are some very special people I wish to thank for their assistance with this volume. First, to my daughters, Rebecca and Rachel, for their loving support.

I would also like to thank the staff of Vision International University for their willingness to follow the Lord first and me second.

To Daniel Romero, my illustrious son-in-law who has helped complete this project.

To Dr. Bohac, who is now with the Lord for his initial editorial expertise and lifelong friendship.

A special thanks to Dr. Greg Wark for his contributions to the text and for allowing me to include his thoughts in this endeavor for the Kingdom of God.

Finally, to the many leaders, good and bad, from whom I have learned and grown through my experiences. I am eternally grateful to each of them.

TABLE OF CONTENTS

PREFACE.. 3

PREFACE TO SECOND EDITION... 5

ACKNOWLEDGMENTS.. 7

CHAPTER 1

  THE NEED FOR LEADERSHIP... 13

CHAPTER 2

  DYNAMICS OF LEADERSHIP.. 39

CHAPTER 3

  SPIRITUAL PRINCIPLES.. 59

CHAPTER 4

  THE LEADER: A LIFE IN BALANCE.. 81

CHAPTER 5

  A CALL TO ACCOUNTABILITY... 95

CHAPTER 6

  THE LIFE OF A LEADER... 103

CHAPTER 7

  A CALL TO SPIRITUAL LEADERSHIP.................................... 117

CHAPTER 8

A CALL TO COMMITMENT..147

CHAPTER 9

CHURCH GOVERNMENT AND ADMINISTRATION........................159

CHAPTER 10

THE LEADER IN RELATIONSHIP..173

APPENDIX 1 195

APPENDIX 2 199

BIBLIOGRAPHY 201

OTHER BOOKS BY THE AUTHOR...203

"Vision without action is merely a dream. Action without vision just passes the time. Vision with action can change the world"
Joel Barker

"A great leader must be an educator, bridging the gap between the vision and the familiar. But he must also be willing to walk alone to enable his society to follow the path he has selected."
Henry Kissinger

"Where there is no vision the people perish" Proverbs 24:18

CHAPTER 1

THE NEED FOR LEADERSHIP

In a conversation with my dear friend and spiritual leader, Ken Chant, he expressed some sentiments on the needs of America. In brief, he stated "With the incredible social, economic, political and spiritual problems in America, the only hope (for her) is a good dictatorship!" Well, perhaps some would see this as an oversimplification, or genuinely appalling, but there is some truth in Dr Chant's words.

Every four years in the United States, a new President is elected who promises "change." It seems our country embraces the reality of our problems, and many believe that a charismatic leader of our representative democracy could make the changes sought. Though I pray for and hope that our President makes positive changes, the truth remains that the problems in our society (or any for that matter) are too great for one man, even if he/she was a benevolent dictator. Our country, as with most nations, is desperate for leaders who can make a difference in industry, business, government, and in the Church. The key to success, in any culture, is to rest on the shoulder of its leaders. More than ever, we need Godly leaders to take serious their call and make an impactful difference.

There are two places or positions where leaders are desperately needed. You may be surprised by my perspective. I list them in priority:

The Family - recent studies indicate that 70% of

marriage partners come from broken homes. Single parent family systems (usually the mother) is becoming the norm. The effects of the absent father, whether due to divorce, death or social withdrawal, is being felt now more than ever. The breakdown of moral values and biblical absolutes leave mother and child without the safety of a healthy boundary. The need for leadership, in proper biblical order (Ephesians 5:1 and 1 Peter 3) is needed, and must become a priority of the Church and nation, if the child is to thrive, and not merely survive.

The Church - Gilbert Cann, in his book *Liberating Leadership* states, "I learned that God places in the hearts, minds, and wills of young believers a strong desire for direction, counsel, help, discernment, support and encouragement of older Christians."[1]

This is especially seen in the inner city. With the absence of leadership in the home, children look to other places for role identification and self-image establishment. How tragic for so many that the models available are seen on T.V. or the silver screen, or worse yet, in the drug pusher, prostitute, or young leader on the block. The church, which should be a haven of rest, a hospital for the hurting, a home for the wayward, is perceived as a cold, heartless institution more interested in one's dress, clichés and offerings than the condition of the soul. This perception is profound and is perpetuated by the media and the Church itself.

The Apostle Paul wrote to Titus (Titus 2) to encourage the older men and older women in the faith to care for the younger. The call of every ministry leader is to "Lead and Feed" the sheep (see John 21). When the church remembers its central focus of establishing the Kingdom of God as

---

[1] Cann, G., *Liberating Leadership*, p 39, 1989

expressed in righteousness (right moral relations with God, self and/or another) peace (tranquillity and rest in God) and joy (happiness and contentment with purpose) through its leaders, and the transformation of society will begin.

Certainly, we need leadership in other areas. We need educators, business executives, politicians, etc. to fulfill Godly expectations for the administration of justice, mercy and humility. If the home and church are functioning as God intended, the leaders, so desperately needed in other fields, would emerge.

It is my belief that leaders are developed in the crucible of relationships; as is biblical character formed in faithful men and women. The character of man is much more important than the charisma and when both are found in proper measure, sprinkled with a large measure of knowledge, understanding, wisdom, and the Spirit of God, dynamic leaders are produced.

Leadership ultimately begins with God and will end with God, and is in His hands at all points in between. God has chosen to work with men (Emmanuel, God with us) to fulfill this glorious purpose. He chooses leaders, and intends success for each one. In any case, He begins in the counsel of his own will, and with a vision.

THE NEED FOR VISION

All leadership, if it is to be effective, must begin with VISION. Vision is the ability to see something accomplished well in advance of the reality. Leaders who are bound to the reality principle are not truly leaders, but managers of someone else's vision. True vision always originates from God in the Christian church.

But Nanus asserts in his book, Visionary Leadership, that being a visionary is the one essential component of great leaders.[2] His focus is on business, but the concept certainly applies to the Church. This would fit closely with Peter's and Waterman's concept of visionary and entrepeneurialship traits in successful leaders. One must know where they are going, if they are going to get anywhere, and for leaders in the Church, this begins with God.[3]

The Process Of Vision

As stated before, vision comes from God. It must be supernaturally discerned by revelation (uncovering of a mystery) in the spirit of man. In God's Word, vision is best taught in Habukkuk 2:1-3, NASB:

> *"I will stand on my guard post and station myself on the rampart; and I will keep watch to see what he will speak to me, and how I may reply when I am reproved. Then the Lord answered me and said, 'Record the vision and inscribe it on tablets that the one who reads it may run. For the vision is yet for the appointed time. It hastens toward the goal, and it will not fail. Though it tarries, wait for it; for it will certainly come, it will not delay.'"*

In this most important passage of Scripture we can observe several aspects of vision. It would be too lengthy to attempt a complete exegesis of the passage, but some cogent commentary is provided.

A Fresh Vision Is Needed

First, in proper context, the prophet had been miserably complaining to God about the spiritual condition of the

---

[2] Nanus, Burt, *Visionary Leadership*, 1990
[3] Covey, S.R., 1990

people of God about the spiritual condition of the people of God. He is questioning God's strategy for his nation in light of their impoverished spiritual condition. Yet, the prophet is acutely aware of his own lack of knowledge and wisdom for the situation. He is crying out to God seeking a "word" from the Lord. He knows instinctively that he is unable to see things clearly as God does; thus a fresh vision is needed. The prophet shows his wisdom in the stance he takes in Chapter 2. Let's take a closer look.

RECEIVING THE VISION

First, the prophet already had a place where he was to stand, a place to keep watch. He already was faithful in service, devoted to duty, open to correction. In other words, he was humble and submissive to the will and work of the Lord, and was determined to fulfill his mission. In the Hebrew, this would be much like a goalie setting himself for the firing of a puck or the catcher setting himself for the runner coming toward him in a home plate collision. He had a firm determination to "see what he will speak" (revelation), and how he would be corrected, so he could see things God's way. Often as leaders we will receive a vision from the Lord, but contained in the vision are midcourse corrections for our own spiritual journey.

WRITING THE VISION

Then it says to record or write the vision, clearly stating what has been given to you from the Lord. This can seem risky, but confession or the telling of the vision, especially in writing, commits us to it. It further releases power for the fulfillment of the vision. It is the leader's responsibility to receive the vision from the Lord (and obviously to have enough maturity and accountable relationships to know if it is a true Holy Spirit-inspired vision or last night's pizza!) and to proclaim it. If it is truly from the Lord, though, it will be tested and others will read it and proclaim it as coming from the Lord, *"spreading abroad the matter"* (Mark 1:45).

PUTTING FEET TO THE VISION

A vision from the Lord contains its own spiritual energy. It is set for a time usually unknown to us, and it will come to pass. We must recognize the vision, write it, proclaim it and possess it. When received from God, a vision becomes a divine obsession, a consuming passion. A leader must have it to truly be a leader. A vision in and of itself must not be kept in a vacuum. We need to move it in a concrete direction or it will die. Let me illustrate.

PURPOSE

From a vision, the purpose of the vision must be developed. A purpose statement is necessary in any organization, taking the vision and putting it into operation. That is, the purpose is what we are about, or why we exist. A purpose is necessary in all areas of our lives, especially the Church.

GOAL

Once a purpose statement is made, specific measurable goals are to be established. Simply, based upon the vision from the Lord and the purpose for your ministry, what goals do you have for long-term and short-term growth? The goals should be clear and tied to actions that can be measured (e.g., add twenty families to the church this year, complete constitution and bylaws for ministry, etc.).

Following the goals come specific plans to fulfill the goals. How are we going to do what we have purposed and have goals for? Who, what, when, where, and how are the necessary questions that must be answered for each goal.

IMPLEMENTATION

I have a dear friend who spends hour upon hour writing and re-writing flow charts, organizational charts, marketing plans, etc. for his ministry. Over the years these elaborate and excellently detailed plans are a monument to his genius, though he has little tangible results to show for it. He has vision, purposes, goals and plans, but has never seen the results he so desires due to lack of or poor implementation.

Implementation means to plan your work, then work your plan. It details what you are going to do, but it mainly **does** it. Talking about work but never doing it, is a sin that leads to starvation (*"...if a man doesn't work, neither shall he eat,"* 2 Thessalonians 3:10). There is no substitute for hard work that is directional. One of my primary difficulties is allowing myself to get side-tracked from the vision God has given, the purposes of our ministry, the goals our team has agreed to, and the plan that we have developed. Plan implementation with constant fixation on the goal set before us brings about the fulfillment of the vision.

EVALUATION

No one is perfect. No leader is perfect. No plan is perfect. Only God is perfect. Thus, we must be open to loving evaluation from others in the Body of Christ. Though painful at times, (especially if it pricks our pride) honest evaluation of a plan and its implementation helps us remain on track. Feedback is needed to ensure that the vision is being fulfilled. Organizations with an autocratic tyrant, which are filled with yes men (co-dependants) will get much done, but in the wrong direction. We need to be accountable to one another. Every pastor needs a pastor, every leader a leader, and objective input from others outside of your control can reduce the need to constantly start over again.

Adjustment

We must make adjustments when called for. This is so because God is always expanding vision, giving new insight and revelation into His purpose for our lives. This necessitates change from the top down.

If a plan doesn't work, and your evaluation says change, change, (there are many ways to skin a cat, I suppose) flexibility is needed. Adjustments are needed when others you have relied upon move in a different direction. Though disappointing, there is no need for despair. If the vision is from God you will have opposition, trials and temptations. But, trust in the Lord, the vision hastens towards the goal (never fast enough for we impulsive visionaries) and it will not fail.

Write The Vision

Because of the importance of writing the vision, I will expound on it. A leader imparts concepts. We, as leaders, share the vision - what God is doing today; His direction, goals and purposes for now and the future. Further, we are to define the problem or need well and provide motivation to those who read. A problem well defined is half solved. We need to define the problem, and provide motive. Motive is that which resides within a person and excites him to action in the promotion of the Lord's work, deepening the lives of those involved. Essentially, people do something because they either want or don't want to. We don't want to motivate people through candy and prizes: "If you do it, I'll give you what you like." This is exterior motivation. God desires that we be self-starters, activated by the Spirit of God. Good leaders recognize that there are different motivators to be used, depending upon person and circumstance. When exposed to various challenges in the real world, leaders must find unique solutions and motivate people to action. Preparation for real life circumstance, and teaching moments in the midst of them, was often seen in the ministry of Christ (see Mark 6:30-50).

Further, we are to provide encouragement for people (1 Thessalonians 5:11, Amplified), as encouragement often motivates people to try new things (Colossians 2:2; 4:8). A negative motivator (do it or else, using guilt, etc.) might work short-term, but not once you turn away. Encouraging people to do personal Word studies helps them grow in faith and prepares them for certain adversity to come.

At times we are to show people how to do things (not just what to do). For example, we teach people to win souls by example (1 Corinthians 4:16; 11:1; 1 Thessalonians 1:6; Philippians 3:16-18). We demonstrate faithfulness through hard work; we are a model for people so they know what is expected of them, thus encouraging them to positive activity.

PAUL'S EXAMPLE

Helen Keller was once asked, "What would be worse than being born blind?" She answered, "To have sight and no vision."

Most successful Christian people, when asked what helped them to achieve their place of success, will invariably speak about a goal, a dream, a mission, something that has motivated them to be what they are for the Lord Jesus Christ.

The world is full of people without a vision. They reach for only those things they can tangibly put their hands on. They aim convenience, never reaching out beyond themselves. They are unable to see themselves as they could be, and rarely achieve the possible.

The poorest person in the world is not a person that is lacking money, it is the person with no vision. Without a dream, a vision, a goal in life, you will never become all that you can become in God.

There is a notable difference between a successful person and an unsuccessful one. A successful person is motivated by a dream that is beyond them. They have a dream bigger than themselves. They have something that keeps them going. It's out of their reach, yet they believe that if they work hard enough and pray long enough, they will one day hold that dream in their hand. That's a SUCCESSFUL PERSON.

An unsuccessful person is only moved by what they see today. They are not tomorrow thinkers. They never look beyond themselves.

THERE ARE FIVE STAGES TO A SUCCESSFUL DREAM (VISION) THEY ARE:

1. **Thought it Stage**: In this stage, we ask the question; Could it be; what would happen if it did?; it's a flash of inspired thought.

2. **Caught it Stage**: After thinking about the dream or vision God gives us, we become excited. What began as a thought grows to contagions and we begin to talk about it, seeing ourselves in that dream.

   Winners and losers go through the first two

stages, but stage three is the difference between a loser and a winner!

3. **Bought it Stage**: After we have thought about that dream for a while, there comes the time to pay a price for it. We must make a deposit to see our dream come true.

This is the difference between a dream and a dreamer. There are unfortunately too many dreamers (who often become schemers) in the church today.

We must settle it within ourselves saying, "If that dream is as good as my eyes, there has to be an investment in my life to make that dream happen." No dream (vision) comes to us automatically. This is the time we buy that dream.

Herein lies the difference: The successful person moves into the third stage of the dream; they buy it. They say, "Yes, I'm willing to pay the price," whereas the unsuccessful person will not take the challenge. Just as the successful person bought it, the unsuccessful person fought it. It's at this stage that they begin to rationalize and say, "The reason why I can't do that or have that is because…" They inwardly fight the dream that God has given them to reach their potential. The person that is unsuccessful stops here. They never buy into their dream; they never become what God wants them to be.

4. **Sought it Stage**: It's at this point that true desire comes. We begin to want the vision so badly that it (the vision) possesses us. We sell out, making it happen as God gives strength. Thus, we must be

certain that our vision is from the Lord, recognizing that God never contradicts His Word. He still expects us to love our neighbor, spend time with our family, enjoy a Sabbath rest, etc. We are to keep a balance. But we also must have our dream!

5. **Got it Stage:** This is the best stage of all. When the dream becomes a reality. When you hold in your hands the results of the vision of God. When God's promises become yours and amen!

GOD'S VISION FOR PAUL

It was Paul's vision of what he had been, what he was, and what he could be that kept him steady during the course of his ministry. Though he never "thought" he would lead the church, he certainly pursued it.

In Acts 26:19, Paul tells King Agrippa, "*I was not disobedient unto the heavenly vision.*" He was saying, "In spite of all the problems that I have had or will have, I've been obedient to the dream God gave me."

The vision that God gave Paul did several things to him. First, it stopped him, and it will stop us:

> "*While thus engaged as I was journeying to Damascus with the authority and commission of the chief priests at midday, O King, I saw on the way a light from heaven, brighter than the sun, shining all around me and those who were journeying with me. And when we had all fallen to the ground, I heard a voice saying to me in the Hebrew dialect, 'Saul, Saul, why are you persecuting me? It is hard for you to kick against the goads.' And I said, 'Who art thou, Lord?' And the Lord said, 'I am Jesus, whom you are persecuting.'*" (Acts 26:12-15, NASB).

If we really have a God-given vision, it will change our focus and direction. We begin to see ourselves in the light of Christ.

Further, we see our position in life; that is who we are, and who we are not. Paul came to a sudden halt in his aggressive pursuit when he encountered the living Christ.

This may be discouraging, especially if we have been pursuing goals contrary to God and His Word. All great men and women must see themselves in a proper light if they are to fulfill God's will.

Paul became acutely aware that persecuting Christians was working against God's plan. This probably more than discouraged him; it must have been devastation. It certainly humbled him. Like Paul, many of us not only see our present position, but we also see our potential. The good news is, God believes in us. God is the Lord that encourages us to become all we can for Him.

Isaiah the prophet had a vision of God. Five things happened as a result of this vision:

1. He saw God - a Holy God.
2. He saw himself for who and what he was - needy, imperfect, living amongst men of unclean lips.
3. He saw others in relation to himself and to God.
4. He allowed God to change him - to cleanse him thoroughly.
5. He began to "stretch" when he said, "Send me!"

Isaiah was willing to fulfill the vision on account of the *"so great salvation"* he had received.

Next, Paul's vision sent him:

> *"But arise, and stand on your feet; for this purpose*

I have appeared to you, to appoint you a minister and a witness not only to the things which you have seen, but also to the things in which I will appear to you; delivering you from the Jewish people and from the Gentiles, to whom I am sending you, to open their eyes so that they may turn from darkness to light and from the dominion of Satan to God, in order that they may receive forgiveness of sins and an inheritance among those who have been sanctified by faith in me," (Acts 26:16-18).

God's dream (vision) will not only stop you, but it will send you to touch others. He was stopped, saw his potential and then he was sent to fulfill a great purpose.

The vision requires that we see ourselves, then that we see others. No one can say that they have effectively fulfilled God's vision until they have begun to positively affect the lives of those around them.

PAUL'S VISION

THE "I BOUGHT IT STAGE"

Once a decision has been made to venture into the arena of vision, setting goals that will affect your life and the lives of others is needed. Here we see that Paul bought his vision, and Paul's vision strengthened him:

"Consequently, King Agrippa, I did not prove disobedient to the heavenly vision, but kept declaring both to those of Damascus first, and also at Jerusalem and then throughout all the regions of Judea, and even to the Gentiles, that they should repent and turn to God, performing deeds appropriate to repentance. For this reason some Jews seized me in the temple and tried to put me to death. And so, having obtained help

from God, I stand to this day testifying both to small and great, stating nothing but what the Prophets and Moses said was going to take place; that the Christ was to suffer, and that by reason of his resurrection from the dead he should be the first to proclaim light both to the Jewish people and to the Gentiles," (Acts 26:19-23).

As Paul stands before Agrippa, he recounts the dangers encountered in his ministry. In verse 22, he says

"Having obtained help of God, the vision has strengthened me."

Paul elaborates on the problems faced and of how it was only the God-given vision that helped him through to victory.

Further, Paul's vision "stretched him" (2 Corinthians 11:24-29):

"Five times I received from the Jews thirty-nine lashes, three times I was beaten with rods, once I was stoned, three times I was shipwrecked, a night and a day I have spent in the deep. I have been on frequent journeys, in dangers from rivers, dangers from robbers, dangers from my countrymen, dangers from the Gentiles, dangers in the city, dangers in the wilderness, dangers on the sea, dangers among false brethren; I have been in labour and hardship, through many sleepless nights, in hunger and thirst, often without food, in cold and exposure. Apart from such external things, there is the daily pressure upon me of concern for all the churches. Who is weak without my being weak? Who is led into sin without my intense concern?"

His vision helped him to become what he never would

have been without it. Paul may have become a religious leader of his day, but he would never have fulfilled the plans of God (and we might not have had the privilege of hearing the gospel) had he not been obedient to the vision of the Lord.

Finally, Paul's vision satisfied him (v 19). In essence, he states, "Now that I look over my life, I'm glad that I was obedient."

The happiest people are not the wealthy and healthy. Those who have found something outside of themselves, bigger than they are, can forget who they are and give themselves entirely to their dream.

VISION IN THE LOCALITY

The need for a proper understanding of vision is best summed up by Proverbs 29:18, "*Where there is no vision the people perish.*"

What the writer is saying is that in situations where the vision of God is not evident the people have no sense of guidance or direction.

Clear vision gives purpose and meaning to the ministry, and provides security and stability. Vision is in many ways like government – it provides the framework that defines the boundaries of safe and fruitful operation.

IDENTIFYING AND DEFINING THE VISION

Before a leader can proceed, he or she must have a clear sense of where God is leading. This is accomplished by time spent with the Lord in prayer and meditating on the Word. There can be many times of discouragement when the only thing that gets the person of God through to victory is the assurance of knowing that what he or she had perceived was from God.

As stated above, a vision that is received must be written down. There is something about writing things down that gives them solidity. In addition, the act of writing things down spurs new thoughts and inspiration of means for accomplishing the task.

There are several reasons for writing down the vision, or mission statement, according to the writers of the Christian Leadership Letter (June, 1984):

- It establishes the ministry's reason for being.
- It places boundaries around the ministry's efforts, thus defining what it will and will not do.
- It describes the need the ministry is attempting to meet.
- It lists how the ministry is going to respond to the stated need.
- It serves as a hook on which to hang the primary objectives of the ministry.
- It forms the basis or standard of practice for the ministry.
- It helps communicate the vision to others.

When writing the vision, several components should be included to provide clarity:

- The purpose for existence.
- What the ministry is attempting to do.
- Whom the ministry is attempting to serve.
- How the ministry will go about it, and
- The limits or area of ministry (geographic, etc).

In this process the visionary should be as specific as

possible, writing down each thought that comes to mind in each category. From these, the purpose, goals, plans, etc. can be established. Clarifying the vision gives all persons involved in a ministry a comprehensive handle on the mission of the organization and the direction in which it is going.

COMMUNICATING THE VISION

All true leaders are effective communicators. The vision God gives must be translated into procurable parts for proper digestion by the church or ministry. It's not always wise to share the whole picture, depending on the maturity level of the congregation or mission. However, communicate you must, in a clear and positive fashion, so the co-laborers with you will be able to proclaim the vision as though it were their own.

The vision must be kept in front of the people, and can often be boiled down to a few short phrases or words. For example, we use *"Taking the Whole Word to the Whole World"* for the Vision International Education Network. Embodied in that phrase is a picture of planting schools, teachers, workers and empowering leaders to do the same. Every vision has its own uniqueness, and is a small part of the whole revelation Jesus has for His Church today.

Faith is needed if others are to "catch the vision." We must believe that God can develop a significant person, for God chooses a man, not for what he is, but for what he will be (Galatians 2:12-22). For example, how you see a man is how he will function. We must not view people as problems, but as persons with honor. Finally, to see the vision proclaimed we must develop a greater sensitivity toward the people we serve.

God's people have significant needs (psychological, yet very spiritual). Knowing these needs will greatly enhance your ministering ability. These needs include:

- To know they belong, and that they are part of the whole, members one of another, workers together (2 Corinthians 6:1).
- To know that they are of value. Sadly, many people live with feelings of inferiority and worthlessness. People are special to God and should be valued by their leader.
- To know that they are making an important and meaningful contribution to something worthwhile (2 Corinthians 8).
- To visualize that they are going somewhere, that what they are involved in is not just spinning wheels and going in circles. They must have vision and hope.
- To have an awareness of security and acceptance.
- To know that they are being understood (that you have heard them, felt and understood their concern).
- To be encouraged toward productivity, that you have a genuine interest in their growth, development and ministry fulfillment (Romans 8:29; Ephesians 4:11-17).
- To know that the leadership is loyal to them, that they will not be forsaken nor betrayed. The level of trust for ministers is close to used car dealers. (This is unfortunate and must be overcome).
- To have overall approval. God's people receive too much disapproval from the world. In God's house, they need approval. We are to honor one another by God's grace (Romans 12:10).

CONCLUSION

Remember that people are not just numbers and never dollar signs. It is the people's relative response that will provide, to a ministry function, growth, and stature. Remember that Christ came to reconcile people unto Himself. We are to evangelize and disciple people so that they can fulfill their destiny in the Lord.

ISAIAH'S VISION

We can all think of characters in God's Word and in the world that had a dream or vision that motivated them to great heights. They could never have fulfilled their vision without help; thus the need to write it so others will run. We can think of Moses, the deliverer of God's people. Caleb was a man of a different spirit. Colonel Sanders, 70 years young, became the chicken king. George Washington Carver at 70 became Secretary of Agriculture. Thomas Edison at 75 invented the mimeograph. John Wesley was still preaching at age 88, while traveling the countryside on horseback.

When Alexander the Great had a vision, he conquered the world. When he lost it, he couldn't conquer a liquor bottle.

When David had a vision, he conquered Goliath. When he lost it, he couldn't conquer his own lust.

Finally, let us look at vision as it affected the prophet Isaiah.

In Isaiah 6, the vision given to Isaiah the prophet is described:

> *"In the year of King Uzziah's death, I saw the Lord sitting on a throne, lofty and exalted, with the train of his robe filling the temple. Seraphim stood*

above him, each having six wings; with two he covered his face, and with two he covered his feet, and with two he flew. And one called out to another and said, 'Holy, Holy, Holy, is the Lord of hosts, the whole earth is full of his glory.' And the foundations of the thresholds trembled at the voice of him who called out, while the temple was filled with smoke. Then I said, 'Woe is me, for I am ruined! Because I am a man of unclean lips, and I live among a people of unclean lips; for my eyes have seen the King, the Lord of hosts.' Then one of the seraphim flew to me, with a burning coal in his hand which he had taken from the altar with tongs, he touched my mouth with it and said, This has touched your lips; and your iniquity is taken away, and your sin is forgiven.' Then I heard the voice of the Lord, saying 'Whom shall I send, and who will go for us?' Then I said, 'Here I am. Send me!' And he said, 'Go, and tell this people: keep on listening, but do not perceive; keep on looking, but do not understand. Render the hearts of this people insensitive, their ears dull, and their eyes dim, lest they see with their eyes, hear with their ears, understand with their hearts, and return and be healed.' Then I said, 'Lord, how long? And he answered, 'Until cities are devastated and without inhabitant, houses are without people, and the land is utterly desolate. The Lord has removed men far away, and the forsaken places are many in the midst of the land. Yet there will be a tenth portion in it, and it will again be subject to burning, like a terebinth or an oak whose stump remains when it is felled. The holy seed is its stump,'" (Isaiah 6:1-13).

From this vision we learn some of the principles of receiving a vision from the Lord and the results that should be seen. Isaiah saw the Lord sitting on His throne, and heard the praise of Him. The holiness of the Lord caused a response in Isaiah, where he acknowledged his condition of uncleanness before the Lord.

A seraphim touched Isaiah's lips with a burning coal, and brought cleansing to him, then in response to the voice of the Lord, "Whom shall I send, and who will go for us?" he responded, *"Here I am. Send me!"* And the Lord said, *"Go!"*

In this passage we see the steps of a vision that leads to our commissioning, which includes awareness of the Almighty, awe of His holiness, acknowledgment of our sinfulness, acceptance of His cleansing, recognition of God's voice, response to the call and release into service. Each is discussed briefly here.

Awareness Of The Almighty

It must be remembered that all things are contained in God. Everything begins and ends with Him. It is God that calls, not man. Isaiah had a distinct vision of the Lord and His glory. Very few men and women of God have had such an experience, but those who are called of God do have a distinct awareness of the presence of God. They have had an encounter with the Lord that is recognizable to the individual.

Awe Of His Holiness

One of the indicators of a man's or a woman's true encounter with the Lord is a sense of awe at God's holiness. Our Lord is holy, and the fear of the Lord is the beginning of wisdom and knowledge. Isaiah recognized how awesome and marvelous the Lord God is, deserving of our continual praise and worship. Awareness of God's holiness changes our priorities, and fixes our focus on God's mercy and His forgiveness of our sinfulness.

ACKNOWLEDGMENT OF OUR SINFULNESS

Isaiah knew that he did not deserve nor could he stand in the presence of the Lord. He was a sinner. A man of unclean lips. He was also aware that everyone he knew was in the same condition. All he could do was throw himself on the mercy of the Lord. One characteristic of a true visionary is not grandiosity and self-exultation, but meekness and humility before the Lord. No leader of merit will remain a leader in God's kingdom unless he/she remembers where they came from, and God's grace and mercy which has saved and called them.

ACCEPTANCE OF HIS CLEANSING

Thank God for His mercy! Thank God for His grace! Thank God for His cleansing! The cleansing of the heart leads to a change in the talk of the servant of God. Further, the cleansing of the servant of God called to ministry brings a longing in the soul and a message that is filled with the fire of God's righteousness. Elijah had the fire of God caught up in his bones, the Day of Pentecost brought tongues and fire, and a true visionary has a message which burns within; a message that has been given by the Lord.

RECOGNITION OF GOD'S VOICE

It is the Lord who gives vision. Though it may not be audible, it is clear. It is often a still, small voice in the inner man that distinctly states God's purpose and plan for life. Leaders must be able to hear the voice of the Lord, spoken through the Word of God, the prophetic word, or in our secret place of prayer, which will move us in obedience to fulfill our destiny in the Lord.

RESPONSE TO THE CALL

There is always a time of testing which comes to the one who is called. Between the call and the commission is our willingness to obey by faith in spite of the possible hindrances.

I am certain that Isaiah had no idea where the call of God would take him. He was willing to accept the call to speak the word of the Lord to the people of his day. Isaiah was no different than any of us, in that he had weaknesses and limitations. Yet, God in His wisdom knows all about the weaknesses of His servant, and where we are weak He will make us strong. Our response is to submit to the call and be willing to say and do what the Lord has called us to. Of course, we must go through preparation (education, training, maturing) before our release.

RELEASE INTO SERVICE

From the time of the call to the time of release can seem an eternity. But the time is never wasted, since our life is in Lord's hands.

When we are finally released into our calling, we are simply to follow the voice of the Lord and be true to the "heavenly vision" just as Paul the Apostle was (Acts 26:19). Our life should demonstrate servant leadership in the Kingdom of God, working out the vision that the Lord has given for the benefit of others.

WE NEED VISION

It is apparent that vision is needed to fulfill God's purposes, thus the Church needs to:

- Pray that God will indeed bring to pass the vision (*Your kingdom come, Your will be done, on Earth...*

Matthew 6:10)

- Picture (envision) that the people will grasp the vision fully.
- Prepare for the fulfillment of the vision through a well defined purpose, plans and implementation.
- Personnel will be needed, since the work cannot be done alone. Co-laborers are needed and must be recruited.

Once the vision is understood, the task of leadership begins in earnest. This will be discussed in the next chapter on Dynamics of Leadership.

My hope is that you will, like the prophet Habakkuk, set yourself to receive a vision from the Lord and proclaim it for the glory of the Lord.

"A leader, once convinced that a particular courses of action is the right one, must be undaunted when the going get tough."
Ronald Reagan

"Leadership is based on a spiritual quality; the power to inspire others to follow."   Vincent Lombardi

"A leader is a dealer in hope."
Napoleon Bonaparte

CHAPTER 2

DYNAMICS OF LEADERSHIP

DIFFERENT MODELS

I was recently in a Walmart Store getting a pair of glasses refitted when I noticed a plaque on the wall. It is something very familiar to any present or former Walmart employee. On it there were listed the seven keys to their management/work philosophy that is to a great extent responsible for their dramatic success. Though I cannot say what the original intention or specific meaning of each point is, I have taken the liberty to provide my own commentary. Here is the list:

- Commitment to excellence, or a passion to do whatever you do to the best of your ability. This is often missing in the Church, which is expected to get along with second best or worse.

- Dedication to the task, and my guess is to each other as well. Thus a sense of "we" is produced or teamwork, where everyone is equally vested in quality and customers' satisfaction.

- Consistency, or doing quality things in a quality manner every time. No chaos, but predictability which breeds confidence and security (and brings customers back again).

- Attention to detail, a favorite military leadership phrase, which means that the small things do matter. A clean work site, a smile, a word of kindness, no detail is insignificant.

- Consistent innovation, creativity is encouraged and rewarded. When a leader releases his/her people to be creative, creative solutions can and will be found.

- No surprises, communication, frequent team meetings, awareness of the big picture is encouraged. An informed crew is a happy one, and is ready for a clear answer to a question from the customer.

- No excuses, if you fail, you admit, submit, and commit. That is, you admit your failure without excuse, you submit to correction and/or make amends if possible, and commit to excellence and its pursuit.

Of course, no organization is able to 100% fulfill each area. But, if a whole group (or church) had the same focus, the growth curve would certainly be expanded. Another view of dynamic leadership can be found in the recent best seller, *7 Habits of Highly Effective People* by S.R. Covey. Though I don't necessarily agree with all of his focus or his philosophy, he makes some excellent points. Here are Covey's big seven:

- Be Proactive (not reactive). You must have personal vision and direction for your life and work. If you are constantly putting out fires, going from one crisis to another, you can never fulfill your calling.

- Begin with the End in Mind. Personal leadership and results orientation are encouraged. This smacks of New Age, but his point is good. You must have something you're shooting for, if you're going to hit the target. Thus, your focus on vision must be future and now.

- First things First. Choices must be made between what is urgent and what is important.
- Think Win/Win, not Win/Lose. Teamwork and mutual benefit networking or co-operative relationships are much more effective than needless competition.
- Seek First to Understand, then to be understood. A leader must learn to be an empathic listener.
- Synergy. A creative cooperation or unity of purpose must be found.
- Sharpen the Saw. A leader must remain balanced, and learn to have balanced self-renewal.

These characteristics were found consistently in top-level leadership across America. Something to ponder.

DYNAMICS OF LEADERSHIP

DEFINITIONS

What is a leader? According to Webster, a leader is one who acts as a guiding force, commander, etc. By definition a leader must be out front, not comfortably behind. Leadership in the office, position, or capacity of a leader; guidance. The ability to lead, exert authority, etc. A group of leaders. Thus, leading is having the capacity and effect of controlling, influencing or guiding. One who, or that which leads; the act of guidance.

A true leader is first a disciple. As a disciple, he/she must:

- Be willing to serve (Mark 10:35-45)

- Be willing to learn (Matthew 16:22-23)
- Have a teachable spirit (Matthew 16:22-23)
- Be submissive to legitimate authority (Hebrews 13:17)
- Be willing to share faith (I John 1:1-13)
- Exhibit humility (Philippians 2:3-4)
- Be forgiving (Matthew 18:21)
- Be persistent and courageous (Ephesians 6:10-18)
- Be trustworthy and responsible (1 Corinthians 4:2)
- Use time wisely (Ephesians 5:15-17)
- Be quick to obey God (Luke 5:4-9)
- Have faith in God, not just faith in faith (Mark 11:20-22)

Leaders can come in all shapes, sizes and colors. Leaders can have different temperaments, come from different cultures, and come from an enriched or a deprived family. As you cannot tell a book from its cover, so you cannot identify a leader simply by the outward appearance.

In Christian circles, true leadership that is led of the Spirit of God should have some distinctive characteristics:

LEADERSHIP TRAITS

More important than the leader's style, personality or giftings, is his character. God is more interested in who we are, than in what we do. Thus, the character or traits of the leader are vital to success from God's perspective. Some of the key qualities of a leader are:

JUDGMENT

Judgment is the quality of logically weighing facts and possible solutions on which to base sound decisions. Enhance your judgment by being as technically qualified as possible. This is an area that can improve when a leader practices making estimates of a situation while anticipating situations that require decisions. Thus, you can be prepared when the need arises, avoid making rash decisions, trusting that the Holy Spirit will give insight. Proper judgment is a characteristic of maturity in the life of the leader.

JUSTICE

The ability to be impartial and consistent in dealing with people is justice. Justice involves the rendering of reward and the meting out of punishment in accordance with the merits of a case. Anger and other emotions must not enter into a leader's decision making. Prejudice of race or creed must be avoided. Few things will disrupt the morale of an organization more quickly than unfairness or partiality of a leader toward a certain person or group of people.

Your decisions relative to people are a test of your fairness. It takes time to build a reputation of fairness. One thoughtless error or injustice can destroy a good reputation that took years to establish.

To administer justice, you must understand human behavior. Study people to learn why certain individuals behave the way they do under certain conditions. Analyze past cases that have been decided and determine what you would have done had you been the one to make the decision. This is a mental process and should never be used as an occasion to criticize the decision of another leader. Fortunately, there are some wonderful tools available to help in understanding the dynamics of human behavior. (See Appendix for more information).

To develop the trait of justice a leader should be fair, consistent, and prompt when making a decision and consider each case on its own merits. Further, correct in private, with dignity, and with spiritual understanding while searching your mental attitudes to determine if you have prejudices. If so, make conscious efforts not to permit them to influence your decisions.

Never punish a group for the faults of an individual and avoid overgeneralizations. Finally, recognize members worthy of commendation or award. Do not be known as one who dispenses criticism only.

Loyalty

Loyalty is the quality of faithfulness to your church, your seniors, subordinates, and associates. This quality alone can do much to earn for you the confidence and respect of your seniors, subordinates, and associates. Your every action must reflect loyalty to your Lord.

To develop loyalty it is essential to be quick to defend others from abuse. Never give the slightest hint of disagreement with orders from your leadership when relating instructions to members. Also, practice doing every task to the best of your ability, and wholeheartedly support your leadership's decisions.

Never discuss the personal problems of your members with others. Be discreet in discussing church problems with individuals not involved.

Tact

Tact is the ability to deal with others without creating offense. In the field of human relations, tact is the ability to say and do the proper thing at the right time. Tact involves the understanding of human nature and consideration for the feelings of others.

Tact is important in all personal relationships. Criticism must be clear, yet constructive. It should not cause discouragement nor detract from the drive and energy of the church member. Every spiritual leader needs to be tactful when advising those who seek counsel on embarrassing personal matters. Avoid passing judgment; your role is primarily that of a counselor. Sometimes the highest degree of tact is simply to listen with understanding interest and permit the member to discover his/her own solution. You may agree with the solution discovered, give an opinion or suggest another way.

To demand courtesy, and to fail to return it in full measure, indicates either arrogance or a lack of interest. Courtesy stems from one's mental attitude and is expressed in both words and actions. One leader may bark out directives impersonally and abruptly. Another may give his directives in a tone tinged with courtesy that implies the expectancy of obedience. Either method may get obedience, but the second of the two will get more willing obedience and cooperation. Usually a calm, courteous, though firm tone of speech will bring a quick response. Thus, tact and courtesy are closely related to a healthy mental attitude as well as to manner and language.

To develop tact, a leader must be courteous and cheerful in his communication to others. Also, he/she must study the actions of ministers who enjoy a reputation for being skilled in human relations.

Develop the habit of cooperating in spirit as well as in fact. Know when to be seen both officially and socially. Anticipate when your presence or absence may embarrass yourself or others.

WISDOM

Solomon prayed for it; Jesus certainly had it; we definitely need it – Wisdom. Wisdom is best defined as the judicious application of knowledge and understanding to solve a practical problem. Jethro's counsel, though not clearly from God, had elements of practical wisdom based upon his knowledge (of Moses, leaders taking on too much responsibility) and understanding (of Moses and the neediness of the people). The apostles used wisdom in selecting Hellenistic Jewish men to solve the Hellenistic Jewish women's complaint in Acts 6. Thus, avoiding a potential church split. Leaders need wisdom to lead effectively, which requires much knowledge, especially about people and much understanding; mixed with godly timing as to what to do and when to do it. Wisdom comes by experience and through prayer. More will be presented on this important topic in Chapter 3.

TYPES OF LEADERSHIP

There are four primary styles of leadership.

1. First is an **Authoritarian Leadership**: this is leadership based on authority vested in the office by biblical or other institutional authority. The authoritarian leader uses his power to exert control, and usually gets what he wants. Unfortunately, this type of authority can destroy relationships, discourage participation and creativity, and limit the growth of ministry to the capabilities of the leader (unless he has unusually large financial and personnel resources).

2. Secondly, there is **Persuasive Leadership**: this is leadership based on the personal influence of the

leader brought to effect by his personality, character, persuasive ability, and dedication to the mission of the organization. The persuasive leader is often well liked, and his charisma can enthuse people toward action. However, if the charismatic leader leaves, even for a short time, the work can stagnate or fail. People need motivation, but cannot survive on that alone.

3. Thirdly, there is **Democratic Leadership**: this is leadership vested in the voting members who elect a representative to lead them. The democratic leader has the benefits of participation without the fear of authoritarian rulership. However, often when Christian ministry is attempted by committee, or when an inadequate leader (or one who is obviously not called of God) is elected, the church can suffer greatly.

4. Finally, there is Theocratic Leadership: which is leadership under the leadership of Christ. Much more will be said on God's government later in this book. The theocratic leader has the Holy Spirit choose leaders, confirmed by other leaders, and set in place for service. When properly done and supported, this is without doubt God's way.

ELEMENTS OF LEADERSHIP

Each leader must formulate his or her own solution for each problem based upon a thorough analysis of the three basic elements in the leadership environment, which are the leader, the group, and the situation.

The leader must analyze himself and develop personal traits and professional techniques that will ensure success in a leadership role.

The group must be understood on the basis of its organizational structure, sub-leaders, cultural background, and educational competencies. It must be viewed also as a grouping of individuals involving personality, emotions, values, desires, etc.

Each situation must be faced as a new and separate problem with its own answer, and there must be a continuous evaluation of the situation as it changes. The fact is that flexibility is needed in leadership.

THE OBJECTIVE OF ORGANIZATIONAL LEADERSHIP

The ultimate objective of leadership is the successful accomplishment of the mission of the organization. The mission may vary, as the vision is expanded or modified. The effectiveness of an organization lies chiefly on the shoulders of the leader.

THE LEADER'S ROLE

The leader must first of all know oneself. It has been said that an unexamined life is hardly worth living (Socrates). To know oneself, he/she must have the mental courage to evaluate personal strengths and weaknesses in terms of moral, physical, and mental characteristics. The leader must seek an awareness of his/her image as viewed by the members of those being led.

Next, the leader must understand and recognize individual differences in the people they lead. Each person has his/her own individual personality and each is affected differently by the aspects of a given environment. The leader must further understand behavioral traits of individuals, so that the proper appeal or approach can be selected which will cause the individual to respond willingly in the way in which the leader desires.

The leader's understanding of human behavior patterns, of individual differences and the drive for satisfaction of basic human needs provides the basis for the establishment of healthy working relationships. The development of desirable group interaction, and the accomplishment of the mission of the ministry will soon follow.

It should be recognized, however, that the leader's goal, the personalities of the people with whom he is working, and the circumstances of the specific situation will have a profound effect on which particular trait or traits needs the most emphasis.

A LEADER INFLUENCE

A primary question many pastors and church leaders ask is, "How can I efficiently move my people in the direction God wants me to take them?" To determine this, consider the following:

Those in leadership have influence and power. Consider the results of leaders' decisions on the people who follow them.

For instance, in Numbers 13, ten spies – ten tribal leaders – **misled a whole nation**. Rather than entering tin to the land of promise, they begin a wilderness wandering. Also, in the Book of Judges we see several cycles of spiritual decline (Judges 2:8, 16; 3:9-15, 28; 4:1; 6:7-8,34; 8:33, etc.) In each case, it was a leader moving in improper motivation that led to disastrous results, both for the leader and the led.

Leadership consists of a sense of decisions that should follow a logical progression. Presented here are the six "Ps" of leadership process for your consideration.

PROCESS OF LEADERSHIP

PURPOSE - What am I trying to accomplish? All leaders must be able to think in a logical manner. The memory components of this process are included here. This is not a one-time question but an ongoing inquiry. More ministries are shipwrecked for lack of focus on the ultimate purpose of its calling.

PLAN - A strategy must be developed. How am I going to achieve my objective? Again, without a positive plan that fits your specific vision you can only expect to fail.

PERSONNEL - You must have a staff. Who can I recruit to help me? Even the Lone Ranger had Tonto. We cannot do things without anointed servants to help us.

PROGRAM -A program is a structure organizing for action. **How** and **when** shall we begin? This includes goals - concrete steps necessary to accomplish your plan.

PROMOTION - The truth is, people need motivation. You must share with enthusiasm the vision, plan and program in innovative ways.

PROGRESS -We must have feedback to ensure that we are accomplishing God's will.

Let me expand on these primary principles and processes.

PURPOSE OF LEADERSHIP

Know where you are going, what you are going to accomplish, and why. Ask yourself how you are to determine objectives. Key questions to ask yourself include:

- What does God want me to accomplish?
- What do I need to accomplish?
- What am I able to accomplish?
- What is my responsibility?
- What is the responsibility of others?
- What is my heart's vision?
- What are the current needs?

Some samples include building:

- a strong base of operation
- a house for God's presence (Eph. 2:20-21)
- a body for Jesus to work through (Eph. 4:16)
- a training camp for soldiers
- a hospital for the sick, wounded and needy
- a supply base

PLANNING IN LEADERSHIP

Most leaders do not spend enough time in planning. Planning will pre-determine your future. The American Management Association suggests senior managers should spend 30% of their time in planning.

IMPORTANCE OF A PLAN

God had a plan in creation (followed one step at a time) and in redemption. Jesus taught the importance of planning (Luke 14:28-32, Matthew 7:24-27). Scripture commends planning and following the plan (Proverbs 16:1, 3, 9; 21:15; Exodus 25:9, 40). Blueprints are important in construction.

A plan enables you to coordinate and direct energy in the most effective way, avoiding purposeless activity (1 Corinthians 9:26).

How To Plan

There is a primary time to seek the guidance of the Holy Spirit. All leadership should, of course, submit themselves to the perfect will of the Lord. In addition to seeking the guidance of the Holy Spirit, a leader should review stated objectives. You should list various aspects, tasks, and jobs; objective breakdown. Next, you need to evaluate your work force and their potential. Then you will match work force with various tasks.

In addition to the foregoing, you must plan your program. Set goals, which are steps in how to best achieve your objective, and to enlist, motivate, and promote people to fulfill the plan. Then you will need to set a target date! Goals are to be clearly established and measurable, including a realistic time frame for their accomplishment, are of paramount value.

Budget

Make sure you "weigh the cost" before launching a project. Be sure to seek experienced counsel before finalizing plans, and make sure you have the resources to complete it.

Personnel In Leadership

Determining and selecting your task force is of utmost importance. However, since the church is people, the best objectives and finest plans are useless without them. Of course, since most workers are volunteers, being a "people person" is a vital skill.

Leaders must become people experts, learning to relate, motivate, correct, encourage, and develop **people**. The focus should be on assisting them to find an effective place of service in the Body of Christ. Helping them to know and function in their gifts can be a key.

CHOOSING PERSONNEL

You must work with what and who you have. An important principle to note is that the Lord knows who you have in your ministry, good or bad, happy or sad, self-motivated, or a plodder (John 17:6, 9, 12).

You must sincerely thank God for each one - Paul certainly did (Ephesians 1:16; 1 Thessalonians 1:2; Philippians 1:3). Pray that every person will stand perfect and complete in the will of God (Colossians 4:12).

In recruiting people, one of the primary scriptural mandates for leaders is to choose faithful people (2 Timothy 2:2): "And the things that thou hast heard of me among many witnesses, the same commit thou to faithful men, who shall be able to teach others also."

Look for spiritual hunger - a worshipper, responsive to the word, a prayer. Look for those who want responsibility rather than authority, whose hearts are fixed on service and not position or fame.

PROGRAM IN LEADERSHIP

Programs mean organizing. Organizing is placing people in a structure in order to accomplish certain goals. It is matching various tasks with your work force, giving detailed job descriptions, guidelines, target dates, and goals, in other words – taking concrete steps to put your plan into action!

ORGANIZATION

There are many ways to organize, but organize you must. Organization entails the development of a detailed plan of action that you intend to use to fulfill objectives. Then you must work your plan.

A major part of the organizational plan is the selection of workers. Usually an interview process is needed for that purpose. Often spiritual leaders have poor or clouded judgment in making these choices due to their mercy gift or other obstacles. Perhaps two interviewers can help. Then you must do placement/delegation - matching the right person to the right job. This can be quite an art form. You could consider the job needs, skills needed, and the personnel they must work with. This is no easy task.

A job description needs to be provided. It is advisable to have the prospective employee assist in writing the job description. This reduces the possibility of misunderstandings and disappointments.

I cannot emphasize enough the need to teach and train. Providing the materials needed to accomplish the task is also an important way of avoiding confusion. Training needs to set goals for achievement. Encourage and motivate them to fulfill their area of responsibility. Set a target date to begin and accomplish the task at hand. Nothing is more discouraging to a worker than to have to rush everything they do. Crisis management as a style is not management at all, just an adrenaline rush!

PROMOTION IN LEADERSHIP

One of the complaints I hear from spiritual leaders in Western nations (that you generally do not hear overseas) is how unmotivated a people can be. Getting your volunteer "Army of God" moving forward can be most difficult for the best of leaders (e.g., Moses!). Motivation starts with a clear vision.

You must communicate that vision with conviction. Convince from Scripture and with examples that God's mandate is upon your work and that they are a vital part in fulfilling the vision. As you share the vision, exude excitement, burden and faith. If you don't believe the vision, neither will they. Also, show how the plan will benefit the individual and the Body to accomplish the goal. Of course, you need to have more than slogans. You must have objective goals that they can help achieve. One way to accomplish this is to enlist people to fulfill an objective rather than a job.

Having a clear mission objective that your people can strive for carries its own energy. Assist people in understanding what you expect and how it needs to be done.

Prepare detailed job descriptions. Show **what** you want accomplished and **how** it needs to be done. As you do so, express genuine confidence in your personnel's ability to accomplish the task. Your confidence in them and frequent encouragement, praise and assistance when needed will keep them motivated. Of course, trust the Holy Spirit to guide you in your leadership.

PROGRESS IN LEADERSHIP

Any good leader must, at intervals, examine his or her progress! Have we reached our goals? Have we moved forward in our objective? Progress will require supervision and oversight, yet with enough trust and wisdom to allow your workers to work.

Why Supervise?

Supervision is needed to keep the plan moving and to maintain the objective. Also, it helps you know when to make adjustments and correction as you plan. No matter how "anointed" a leader you are, not <u>all</u> of your plans will succeed. Adjustments are a frequent part of life. Supervision develops workers and exposes neglect. If there is a lack of faithfulness in completing tasks responsibly, your oversight can correct it. Thus, it encourages faithfulness and diligence and places importance on the immediate assignment.

How To Supervise

Oversight:

> "Feed the flock of God which is among you, taking the oversight thereof, not by constraint, but willingly; not for filthy lucre, but of a ready mind." (1 Peter 5:2).

Supervision requires the establishment of standards of performance: what you want done, how you want it done, etc. More time is needlessly wasted due to a lack of understanding of what is expected. Arrange regular interviews to examine, discuss, and encourage your co-laborers with their work. Make corrections and confront with gentleness, and ensure the dignity of the individual. Part of that occurs when you work to determine alternative solutions to problems that occur.

When I was stationed in the Army at Fort Leonard Wood, Missouri, we had a commanding general who had earned the respect of all his staff and soldiers. He was, of course, extremely busy, but he always found time to periodically "walk through" to see how his various charges were doing. He showed general interest in what we were doing, through he probably had no real idea of our daily tasks. His example kept us on our toes as we knew the "boss was watching." He was rarely critical, genuinely interested, and positive in approach. He was indeed an example for us to follow.

How To Write Job Descriptions[4]

Every worker needs to know what he is required to do and what standards of performance are expected of him. A written job description is best. The components of a good job description include:

- Title – identifies the job that is to be accomplished.
- Purpose – how it relates to the overall objective.
- Responsibilities – every required duty spelled out. It helps to involve the worker in preparing the job description.

The responsibilities should be spelled out, including:

- Specific responsibilities in order of priority
- Required standards of performance
- Delegated authority and accountability
- The reports that are required and when they are due

When a person decides that the Lord would be blessed by his or her working in the ministry, they deserve our best. How we motivate, train, and develop our "gifts from God" will determine our success in our calling.

---

[4] For more, see *Managing the Kingdom* by Stan DeKoven.

"The quality of a leader is reflected in the standards they set for themselves." Ray Kroc

"Leadership is doing what is right when no one is watching." George Van Valkenburg

"The Lord looked and saw that there was no justice. He was appalled that there was no one to intervene."
Isaiah 59:15-16, RSV

CHAPTER 3

SPIRITUAL PRINCIPLES

Leadership requires of the leader many things, the most important of which is wisdom. The word "wisdom" in the original Hebrew means to pound something in. Its importance is seen in God's Word.

> "The **fear of the Lord** is the beginning of wisdom and the knowledge of the Holy One is understanding," (Proverbs 9:10).
>
> "The **fear of the Lord** is the beginning of wisdom, a good understanding have all those who do his commandments," (Psalm 111:10)

Wisdom is comprehending the basic meaning of life. God's words are spirit and life (John 6:63). God's words are life and health (Proverbs 4:20, 22). God's words are life and godliness (2 Peter 1:3). We can expect to grow in wisdom just as Jesus did, if we "do it" just as Jesus did! He had a spiritual calling, "*I must be about My Father's business*" (Luke 2:49), and He was determined to fulfill the call.

It wasn't until He made Himself subject to His authority (parents) and left His spiritual ministry at the temple, that the Bible has this to say; "*... and Jesus increased in wisdom and stature, and in favor with God and men*" (Luke 2:52). If Jesus grew, how much more do we need to grow in all aspects of our lives?

Wisdom was asked for by Solomon, and is part of the seven-fold Spirit of God (Isaiah 11:1). Wisdom is defined as the ability to discern from God's perspective the correct course of action in a given situation, and requires understanding, sensibility and the ability to delineate between holy and unholy. Wisdom is not just common sense, (though that is certainly helpful) but is a God-given characteristic needed in every leader's life. If it is lacking, prayer and submission to elder ministers for counsel is strongly urged.

Wisdom is obtained or begins with the fear of the Lord (Proverbs 9:10, Psalm 111:10). That is, we must remember that God is sovereign, holy, majestic, all powerful and awesome. Western society frequently demonstrates a lack of proper respect for the house of God and His leader. This must be recaptured, modeled by leaders in their daily conduct. The fear of the Lord is developed as we submit to the work and will of the Father, even as Jesus did in His earthly ministry.

ADDITIONAL SPIRITUAL PRINCIPLES

The Word of God lists several spiritual qualities which qualify men for leadership among God's people. The Scripture emphasizes character above ability. There are many gifted and capable people who desire leadership, but who are unqualified because of lack of spiritual character. In God's Word we find that His chosen leaders often faced obstacles that in the natural seemed beyond solution. Of course, God always proved Himself strong when His servants called upon Him. However, the Bible also points out the failed attempts by His servants when they chose a good idea versus a God idea, or something clearly ordained by God. As spiritual leaders we have the discretion to act according to our sanctified judgment, yet it is best to "hear from the Lord." There are two primary examples of this premise seen in the life of Moses.

If Moses was to survive the load that was on him for leading and caring for the people of God, he needed men of highest quality. In Exodus 8:17-23, Jethro gives his poignant and still relevant advice. Moses was to focus on prayer and the ministry of teaching the statutes of God to the people, including practical living theology. He was then to select faithful men who fear God, love the truth, hate dishonest gain, and have wisdom and judgment to counsel the people. In other words, he sought co-laborers who were filled with integrity and with a sense to know when to refer the "heavy cases" to Moses. Of course Moses did what his father-in-law counseled, which didn't end his problems, but certainly eased his load.

Let us analyze Jethro's counsel from another perspective. Firstly, there is no indication of the motivation of Jethro's heart. However, we can assume that he had a love for his daughter, at least. I am certain he did not want his daughter returning home due to Moses' premature death. Further, there is no indication that Moses was anywhere near "burn-out." He certainly did not register a complaint with the Lord, nor did he cry out for help. This was a good idea but perhaps not God's best in this circumstance.

Further, it is not unkind to ask a few other questions that in hindsight might have affected Moses' decision. For instance, one should naturally question Jethro's qualifications as a spiritual advisor. Yes, Jethro was a spiritual man. In fact, he was a priest…a Midian. As a priest of the Midianites he would use various spells and incantations to appease evil spirits and incur favor with good ones (animism). Specificly, the name Midian means "confusion." Certainly, the advice of Jethro eventually created grave concern leading to confusion for Moses and the people.

Secondly, one might ask, "Just who were these nearly 10,000 leaders that were created by fiat?" In fact, these men were former slaves, only weeks removed from Pharaoh's administration. Like prisoners running the prison, former slaves could be harder on their own than Pharaoh's professionals. Truly, a good idea may not be the best idea, especially if it is not God's idea.

In contrast to this, we see a different story in Numbers 11:10-17. It reads:

> "Then Moses heard the people weep throughout their families, every man in the door of his tent: and the anger of the Lord was kindled greatly; Moses also was displeased. And Moses said unto the Lord, 'Wherefore hast thou afflicted thy servant? And wherefore have I not found favour in thy sight, that thou layest the burden of all this people upon me? Have I conceived all this people? Have I begotten them, that thou shouldest say unto me, Carry them in thy bosom, as a nursing father beareth the suckling child, unto the land which thou swearest unto their fathers? Whence should I have flesh to give unto all this people? For they weep unto me, saying, Give us flesh, that we may eat. I am not able to bear all this people alone, because it is too heavy for me. And if thou deal thus with me, kill me, I pray thee, out of hand, if I have found favour in thy sight, and let me not see my wretchedness.' And the Lord said unto Moses, 'Gather unto me seventy men of the elders of Israel, whom thou knowest to be the elders of the people, and officers over them; and bring them unto the tabernacle of the

*congregation, that they may stand there with thee.
And I will come down and talk with thee there:
and I will take of the spirit which is upon thee, and
will put it upon them: and they shall bear the
burden of the people with thee, that thou bear it
not thyself alone.'"*

Moses finally hit his "wall." Not only was Moses angry, but so was God. Moses finally cried out to the Lord for a solution to the needs of the people, and God gave him an idea that would solve the dilemma. Not only did God instruct Moses to raise up seventy elders, (apparently the leaders that Moses initially chose did not ease his burden), but God anointed the seventy with the prophetic anointing that was on the life of Moses. These men were Spirit empowered, which is the ingredient that separates good from God.

In the New Testament, we see a similar event occurring in the Church. In Acts 6, the Apostles grappled with a very sensitive problem that could have had serious ramifications for the growth of the Church. The Church was growing dramatically. Until this time the apostles were carrying the entire load of ministry, both in preaching/teaching and administration. The burden became overwhelming with the pressure coming to a head over a dispute between the Hellenistic Jews and the native Hebrews. Apparently in the distribution of food, the Hebrew widows were being better cared for than the Hellenistic Jewish widows. In verse two we see the Apostles wisely calling the whole congregation (probably leaders) together. They stated:

*"It is not desirable for us to neglect the word
of God in order to serve tables. But select from
among you brethren, seven men of good*

> *reputation, full of the spirit and of wisdom, whom*
> *we may put in charge of this task. But we will*
> *devote ourselves to prayer and to the ministry of*
> *the word."*

Thus, their crisis was averted when proper delegation occurred.

When a church is founded on the apostolic ministry, the need for deacons (servants) is usually much greater than elders. More will be discussed on this in the section on five-fold ministry and team ministry. It became imperative for the apostles to find help. But, note the qualifications for becoming servants. They had to be of good reputation. That meant that their spiritual and natural lives would have to be above reproach, men of integrity, ready to work. Second, the Holy Spirit and especially wisdom had to be a recognizable part of their daily walk. Finally, they had to be "take charge" men, not just "yes men." The apostles wanted (and achieved) complete abdication from the "widow" business. These men had to be of the highest quality inside and out.

Later on, as the Church continued to grow, the need for qualified leaders (elders, deacons, and ministries) were needed. Paul the Apostle addressed his young pastors Timothy and Titus and presented the necessary qualifications for spiritual leadership.

Paul had written to Timothy that he needed faithful men (2 Timothy 2:1-6), men who are dependable, diligent and trustworthy. Proverbs 25:19 states: *"Confidence in an unfaithful man is like a broken tooth."* Further, Luke 16:10-12 says *"He that is faithful in that which is least is faithful also in much..."*

True faithfulness will be evidenced in small things, not

just in great assignments (Matthew 25:21). Many will long for greatness but are unwilling to serve their brothers and sisters. In 1 Corinthians 15:46 we see that faithfulness must be proved in natural things before it will develop in spiritual things. Also, faithfulness must be seen in matters of money. Nothing reveals a man's faithfulness more than his handling of money, his diligence in paying bills; it shows his priorities. Stewards are required to be faithful and in order to give account, they must diligently keep accounts. If a man is slothful at home or work, can we expect more in "God's house?" [5]

Also, respect for other's property is taught throughout Scripture. (Ezekiel 34:6-10; Matthew 21:41; 1 Corinthians 4:2; 1 Timothy 1:23; Jeremiah 48:10). As a child, I would receive at least a stern correction, if not a spanking, for sitting on a man's car, crossing someone's yard without permission, etc. How things have changed, but our respect for others should not.

Paul's word to Timothy also indicates that the Lord needs able men and women. This refers to an ability that God gives. Gifted men with special grace endowments are to be searched for to be co-laborers. This includes (Ephesians 3:7; 4-7), "the gift of grace," special gifts (1 Peter 4:10), a wise builder (1 Corinthians 3:10) and gifts according to the measure of faith exercised in humility (Romans 12:3-6).

Further, faithful men are unentangled men, thus having liberty to minister in God's house. This is a man of resolute priority (Matthew 6:33). Further, they are focused on the task (Philippians 2:13) and will bear fruit from their labor. Entangled men do not bear fruit (Luke 8:14), let alone fruit that will stand the tests of time and trial.

---

[5] See Living Fruitfully and Resokdnf your Vision.

Faithful men are submitted men. They are submitted to authority because they are under authority (Matthew 8:9). Further, they are men who learn to follow before they are entitled to lead (Hebrews 13:7). Also, men of character are living examples: (*"Take heed to thyself - then the flock."* Acts 20:28; 1 Timothy 4:10). They lead by example. They exhibit the qualities that are necessary for others to follow (Philippians 3:17; 1 Thessalonians 1:6-7; 2 Thessalonians 3:7-9; 1 Timothy 1:16; Titus 2:1-5; 3:1-2, 8-11, 14; 1 Peter 5:3; 1 Timothy 4:14-16).

They work to be a model of Christian believers in lifestyle, home, business, and ethics. They are not perfect, but are showing victory in the primary avenues of life. Also, they are well disciplined, with mannerly (again, not perfect) children (1 Timothy 3:4-5). Their children are being nurtured in the Lord's admonition (Ephesians 6:4). When the need arises to discipline, "the rod" of correction is lovingly applied, which brings correction to their children. All correction is to be done in love, not to shame or humiliate our children. Family life must be considered in leadership selection.

God is love and we should be gentle men (2 Timothy 2:24). Christ is our example of true gentleness and humility. In many Christian circles, aggression, power and charisma are seen as the most desirable traits of leaders. Yet, Jesus exhibited gentleness and humility even when acting strong and forthrightly. Macho men, if molded into men of God, can carry the quiet strength of meekness that Christ did. Gentleness, humility and meekness are not signs of weakness, but Godly character.

Committed men (2 Corinthians 8:5) are needed in leadership. They are to be wholly committed (1 Timothy

4:14-15; Numbers 32:11-12; Matthew 22:23; Revelation 3:15; Jeremiah 48:10). They are committed to the will of God (Colossians 4:12), the vision of the Church (Acts 26:19), the Body of Christ, especially in its local expression, and to the leadership as Elijah was with Elisha and David's men were to the king. Ultimately, servants are needed before leaders can emerge. Leaders or potential leaders must learn to serve before exercising authority (Proverbs 15:33). Christ again is our example, as seen in Matthew 20:25-28. Many desire positions, recognition, and authority. Leaders should look for men who **desire to serve**. The true Shepherd gives His life for the sheep.

Definitely they must be full of the Holy Spirit (Acts 6:3). The Church is not just a business; it is a spiritual entity and requires wisdom, anointing, and the guidance of the Holy Spirit. Men of only natural ability are not adequate for leadership in the Kingdom of God (1 Corinthians 2:12-15). Men full of the Spirit are men of devotion to God, men of prayer, and faith.

Repeatedly in the Word of God it is recorded that men became great leaders when the Holy Spirit came upon them (Joshua 34:9; Judges 6:34; 15:14; 1 Samuel 10:6-7, 9-10; 16:13).

No one should attempt to become a leader unless the hand of God is upon their life. Many have received Christ (have his image), but have yet to be molded into His character (likeness). This is to be accomplished before we are to work in His vineyard (see Genesis 1:26-27).

The character needs of leadership are so important, we will continue to look at key qualifications for leadership.

Qualifications of Leadership[6]

First of all, the leader must have a good heart. The definition of the word "heart" to the Western mind includes the emotions or feelings of a person. We think of someone loving another with all their heart. To the Hebrew or Eastern mind, it encompassed not only a person's emotions, but also his spiritual, mental, and physical life as well. In the light of the ministry, the Hebrew word *labab* would mean that a person would be involved or committed from the very center of his being. The heart is the seat of his collective energies. The focus of his personal life. To the Greek mind the word *kardia* carries the connotation of both soul and mind. It is the inner life and character of an individual, it is the entire personality, character, body, mind, emotions, and spirit of a person that constitutes what is required.

Character Qualifications

The Balance Between Gift And Character

The Lord's purpose for man is stated in Scripture, in Genesis 1:26-28, "*And God said let us make man after our own image, in our likeness and let them have dominion.*" Paul states in Galatians 4:19, "*I travail in birth until Christ be formed in you.*" and 2 Timothy 3:17, "*That the man of God be perfect.*" The purpose of God for man has not changed. The character and personality of the Lord Jesus Christ must be developed in the Church's leaders before it can be developed in His people.

A balance between gifts and character is the Lord's will for every true leader of God. The imbalance of gifts in leaders versus character has caused many problems in the

---

[6] The author is grateful to Dr. Greg Wark for inclusion of some of his cogent thoughts in this next section.

Church. Many media Christians are considered to be a laughing stock by those who see their lack of character. God is concerned not only with a leader's gift and anointing, but also his lifestyle and character.

The character is the seat of one's moral being. Character can be seen as the action of an individual when under pressure. Also, character is the combination of qualities distinguishing a person.

Character is not only how a person acts, but it is also his motives and attitudes. Character is not measured without everyday disappointments, irritations, and pressures – weaknesses are exposed when the negative occurs. Character is not only having wisdom to know what others should do according to Bible principles, but also living in harmony with those principles for oneself. Character is not only how a person treats other Christians; it is also how he treats other people, whether they be of another culture, race, or religion. Character is not only how a person relates to his spiritual family, but also how he treats his natural family.

Character is developed through the "dealings of God." This is primarily seen when the believer lacks the discipline to develop his character, the Lord will provide learning experiences and circumstances to help him. If the Body of Christ is going to be developed in character through the dealings of God, leaders must be the first to allow God to change their character. This most often occurs during the wilderness experiences common to all believers.

THE HEART OF A LEADER

As a minister or leader in God's house, you will minister to many different types of people and be used by God in wonderful and often dramatic fashion. You will lay hands on the sick and see them recover. You will drive out demons and comfort the brokenhearted. You will lead many to Jesus as their personal Lord and Savior and you will restore many others to their first love for Christ. You will lead men and women into the baptism in the Holy Spirit and free others from the burden of unforgiveness. God's anointing will rest on your life. Please remember that in the midst of all these wonderful things that we are SERVANTS and VESSELS. We are serving our Master, Jesus Christ; and we are serving the people to whom we minister.

One of our primary values is that our lives – that is our thoughts, our words, our bodies, our souls and spirits, are to be set apart and consecrated to Jesus. We are missing the mark if we are healing the sick and winning the lost but at the same time harboring resentment or living in rebellion toward our family or fellow-workers.

AS MINISTERS WE ARE TO:

> *"Do everything without complaining or arguing, so that you may become blameless and pure, children of God without fault in a crooked and depraved generation, **in which you shine like stars in the universe as you hold out the word of life...**"* (Philippians 2:15-16).

One primary characteristic of a heart sold out to the Lord is consecration, or being set apart for Jesus. Though we were all sinners, the Word now calls us saints. What is a saint?

> *"Paul, an apostle of Jesus Christ by the will of God, to the saints which are at Ephesus, and to the faithful in Christ Jesus..."* (Ephesians 1:1).

The word for "saint" in Greek is *hagios*, which means

one who is set apart. Paul addressed believers as saints because we are called to live a life which is set apart, an exceptional life reflecting the beauty of God's holiness. Paul talks of God as one *"Who has saved us, and called us to a holy life,"* (2 Timothy 1:9).

So then, what is holiness? Holiness is much more than the omission of certain behaviors, words and practices from one's lifestyle. Jesus called us to a holiness like the holiness of his Father. He said...

> "Be perfect, therefore, as your heavenly Father is perfect," (Matthew 5:48).

God's holiness is rooted in His character. That which is His nature, is holy. To paraphrase Dr. Ken Chant, theologian, prolific author and dynamic Bible teacher, holiness can be defined as being and doing all God requires of you at a certain place of maturity in your walk. Holiness is not a standard, but a progressive development of Christ-likeness. We should be more holy at the end of our Christian walk than when we start. It is impossible for God to be anything other than holy and so the things which He does are unavoidably pure. They are a constant source of blessing. Do not compromise this standard for your life. The more we compromise in this area, the harder it becomes for God to convict us by His Spirit, and inevitably we will stop growing in God. The end result will be that we will reach a ceiling in our effectiveness in the Kingdom.

Holiness and gifting are to be molded together. It is easy to become either too busy or too prideful to listen to the message of separation and thus lose the urgency of God's call on us to live holy lives. God's heart is to enlarge us, deepen us so that He can pour more and more of Himself into us. As a result we will be able to pour more and more of

Him into a lost world. Remember, the issue is not how gifted we are, God can easily give us more gifts; the issue is how consecrated we are. God has made us righteous through the blood of Jesus, and it is our responsibility, our choice, to pursue the work of sanctification, or setting apart, in our lives. It is much easier for God to pour out gifts than it is for us to relinquish pride and be a "forever learner," humbly submitted to the Lordship of Christ.

Consecration is God's unchanging desire for us. Holiness was a standard which God held for His people, Israel. Note that He did not give complicated reasons why they should be holy, this was a simple command to be followed:

> "I am the Lord who brought you up out of Egypt to be your God. Therefore be holy because I am holy" (Leviticus 11:45).

Though we are in a time of God's abundant grace and mercy, His heart has not changed. He has covered us with the righteousness of Christ, but He still desires that, from a committed and obedient heart, we purpose to live humble and sanctified lives.

> "But just as he who called you is holy, so be holy in all you do; for it is written 'Be holy, because I am holy'" (1 Peter 1:15-16).

As always, Jesus is our example of a consecrated and holy life.

"...anointed with the oil of gladness above (his) fellows" (Hebrews 1:9), because HE LOVED RIGHTEOUSNESS AND HATED INIQUITY.

Further, we are called to live the same way. "Whoever

claims to live in him must walk as Jesus did." (1 John 2:6). Thoughtfully, we are empowered to live this way:

> *"His divine power has given us everything we need for life and godliness through our knowledge of him who called us by his own glory and goodness. Through these he has given us very great and precious promises so that through them you may participate in the divine nature and escape the corruption in the world caused by evil desired"* (2 Peter 1:3-4).

Holiness is not something we gain by self-effort, but by yielding our lives to the Word and the Spirit.

WE ARE TO AIM AT LIVING THIS WAY:

> *"Not that I have already obtained all this, or have already been made perfect, but I press on to take hold of that for which Christ Jesus took hold of me"* (Philippians 3:12).

As leaders, we are to be motivated towards consecration and should motivate others towards the same in our preaching, teaching and lifestyle:

> *"Finally, brothers, goodbye. **Aim for perfection**, listen to my appeal, be of one mind, live in peace. And the God of love and peace will be with you"* (2 Corinthians 13:11).

Remember, consecration does not just happen as we get older. We must make a conscious choice of our will and purpose in our hearts to live a life which is **wholly** pleasing and acceptable in the sight of God:

> *"Having therefore these promises, dearly beloved, let us **cleanse ourselves** from all*

*filthiness of the flesh and spirit, perfecting holiness
in the fear of God"* (2 Corinthians 7:1).

We must be determined to let Jesus wash all the world
away from us and thus consecrate our lives to him **all** day
and **every** day. *"**Make every effort** to live in peace with all men,
and to be holy"* (Romans 12:8).

We must be completely open to the Spirit of God to
enable him to cleanse us, change us, and bring us to full
maturity in His timing.

James exhorted the Church to live lives with actions
which matched their confession of faith. Talking to justified
believers he said:

> *"Come near to God and he will come near to
> you. Wash your hands you sinners, and purify
> your hearts, you double minded"* (James 4:8).

Our greatest productivity and highest measure of joy
comes when our lives are **completely open** to the Lordship
of Jesus. When we are open to His correction as well as His
embrace, we will reject "hidden agendas." As a result, we
will become uncompromising and single minded.
Consequently we will enjoy the Kingdom of God to the
fullest extent; righteousness, peace and joy in every part of
our being (Romans 14:17). As we walk in a consecrated
fashion, clothed in God's holiness, we become in actuality
what we are by position; overcomers in Christ.

The Apostle John did not write to the early Christians
with an attitude that it was inevitable that they were going
to sin. When John wrote he said:

> *"My dear children, I write this to you so that **YOU
> WILL NOT SIN**,"* (1 John 2:1).

John wrote clearly about the unsaved world:

> *"We know that we are children of God, and that the whole world is* **under the control of the evil one**" (1 John 5:19).

John also wrote that in the Kingdom of God life changes. He states: "I write to you, young men, because you have overcome the evil one" (1 John 2:13). Understand that this is not only a Scripture to be confessed, it is a Scripture to be LIVED. John describes how these men were living a life **applying the victory** Jesus had won for them. He says, *"I write to you young men because you are strong, and the word of God lives in you, and you have* **overcome the evil one,**" (1 John 2:14).[7] This victorious living comes through much spirit-filled effort as we *"Continue to work out (our) salvation with fear and trembling,"* (Philippians 2:12).

John declared that Jesus came to destroy every work of the devil in our lives, and to transfer us into a completely new life. This new life distinguishes us from the world system. The result of our new life is that we will bear much fruit. *"The reason the Son of God appeared was to destroy the devil's work"* (1 John 3:8).

Consecration means surrendering who we are to God. That includes **keeping a correct emphasis.** The focus of the holiness historically taught has been on **external behaviors and dress,** rather than on issues of the heart. As we fall in love with God, a deep motivation comes from the Holy Spirit to become pleasing to God. Holiness becomes a deeply sought after necessity for daily life. This desire is not developed by doing things for God, it is developed by fervent prayer. Gradually external behaviors begin to

---

[7] See *Journey of the Kingdom.*

change, because of a heart filled with holy fear, reverence and a deep respect for the mighty God we serve.

As God stirs us to live a holy life, we will find that the issues of our heart change. At first, it seems as though we are constantly changing **what we do**, (God speaks to us about coarse jesting, movies, spending money, etc.), but this is just the beginning. Soon the issue is **who we are**. We experience embarrassment in prayer as God shows us a behavior or thought pattern which is grievous to Him. We realize yet again, that we need to **be like Him**.

Other important characteristics of a consecrated life include boldness, supernatural help, discernment, single-mindedness and greater light. Living a consecrated life increases our **boldness**. We are not held back by guilt, unworthiness or the burden of undealt-with sin. This releases liberty to minister without fear. Living a consecrated life increases the measure of **supernatural** help that we are able to give. If our lifestyle does not grieve the Holy Spirit but rather pleases Him, we will always be open to His counsel, His wisdom, and the flow of His power. Living a consecrated life leads to a **greater** conviction of the darkness of Satan's kingdom and the light of God's Kingdom. As we understand that what we are warring against is darkness and not just social problems (for example divorce or depression), our assurance will increase in our prayers. Our faith and determination will increase as we experience a more powerful ministry. Living a consecrated life will lead to a sense of **anticipation** in our heart as we prepare to minister to someone. Nothing will be distracting us from the ministry God has called us to.

We are in the world to change it: Jesus told us that we are the **light of the world** and the **salt of the earth** (Matthew

5:13-14). This means that we are to preach the gospel, lay hands on the sick, and minister to the needy. Furthermore, by the power of the Holy Spirit we can show the world a life of supernatural beauty in all of our actions. How does the "man of the world" get ahead? By ambition, seizing every possible opportunity for advancement by "looking out for number one." How do we proceed in life? We can be the light of the world by living the truth that:

> *"...For not from the east, nor from the west, Nor*
> *from the desert comes exaltation; But God is the Judge;*
> *He puts down one and exalts another* (Psalm 75:6-7).

We can be the light of the world by living in the supernatural dynamic of servanthood and consideration of others above ourselves. How does the world deal with criticism? By counter attack and vicious conversation. How do we deal with this opposition? By taming our tongues (James 3), and by praying for those who oppose us; this light-life brings tremendous peace and shines freedom onto the dark world around us. Further, God has called peacemakers...the world is contentious place, but we have self-confidence in the Holy Spirit.

We are called to be zealous...in the world there is a lot of disillusionment and apathy.

We are to be gentle...in the world anger rages.

We are to love each other and care for each other as different parts of the same body...the world is often independent and selfish.

We are called to live a life in the Spirit, which brings one of the greatest gains of godliness; contentment...the world is restless and never satisfied, but we have a rest in Jesus Christ.

TO LIVE A CONSECRATED LIFE IS TO BE WILLING TO ALLOW THE HOLY SPIRIT TO REVEAL TO US THE QUALITY OF LIFE HE DESIRES FOR US, NEVER DEFENDING OUR FLESHLY NATURE WITH PRIDEFUL RESISTANCE, BUT ALWAYS RECEIVING HUMBLY THE WORD WHICH GOD WANTS TO PLANT IN US.

"The heart of the wise inclines to the right, but the heart of the fool to the left."
Ecc. 10:2

"It is amazing what you can accomplish if you do not care who gets the credit."
Harry S. Truman

"Leadership is practiced not so much in words as in attitude and in actions."
Harold S. Geneen

CHAPTER 4

THE LEADER: A LIFE IN BALANCE

*"And Jesus grew in wisdom and knowledge,
and in favor with God and man"* (Luke 2:52).

SPIRITUAL

Jesus grew in all aspects of His life: mentally, socially, physically and spiritually. He did so in perfect balance. He was not a physical "macho man," nor was He so spiritually minded that He was no earthly good. As with Jesus, our supreme example, we are to grow up in Him, in a balanced fashion if we are to enjoy long-term effectiveness. Let us briefly examine some of the areas of balance and potential imbalance in a leader's life.

A leader's relationship with the Lord is built upon character as well as depth through God's Word and prayer. Recent surveys indicate that less then 25% of pastors have a daily devotional life, separate from studying for sermons, and Bible studies. Most would indicate how vital spiritual development is, yet find it difficult to cultivate the basics of spiritual discipline.

PERSONAL

The habits, lifestyle, and patterns which a leader adopts will have a profound influence upon the effectiveness of the ministry they have from the Lord. Decisions on personal habits must be made based upon the Word of God and personal conviction; a consistent righteous lifestyle is a positive example to God's people.

THE HOME

Probably the most difficult and affected area of a leader's life is his home life. A leader's family life will be the basis for ministry to the family of God. A leader should have his own home in order which requires work, prayer and grace (1 Timothy 3:4).

MARRIAGE

A leader's marital life will only be successful as he continues to mature and develop character. A man or woman without a developed character will bring his character deficiencies into the home. His/her spouse must also develop in maturity in order for the relationship to be healthy. A leader's marriage will only blossom if character is cultivated, otherwise, he/she will never consistently meet the needs of his/her spouse. For more on the importance of marriage and family in ministry, see *Pastoral Leadership* and *Marriage & Family Life*, both by this author.

SOCIAL

A leader's friends and friendships reflect the character of the leader. A leader must develop sills in relationship building in order to have successful social relationships. Loyalty and acceptance are two factors required in friendship. If a leader has character, they will have the needed elements for a consistent social life. Leaders can tend to be loners. A social life is needed to keep perspective on the "real world." (Remember, Jesus was a friend to "sinners").

EDUCATIONAL

Education by itself is not enough to build good character. Education can be a powerful force in the life of a leader and good character will enable a leader to benefit from an education, in as well as out of the classroom. Continuing education through cultivating good reading habits will stimulate the leader's mind and vision.

MINISTERIAL

The work of a leader who is in an Ephesians 4:11 (five-fold) gift ministry will find that character is the very focus of all that they do. Ministry function is, in itself, a manifestation of a leader's character. What he/she is will manifest in what he/she does in ministry. All five-fold ministry leaders must meet the requirements for elders (1 Peter 5:1).

FINANCIAL

Jesus Christ said if a man could not manage money, God would not commit to him the true spiritual riches of the kingdom. A leader's wisdom, true desires, values, self-esteem, and ability to give are all demonstrated, not necessarily by how much money is earned, but by how it is used and managed.

Many men and women of God have been disqualified from the ministry through weaknesses in areas stated above that have been exploited by Satan. No human being is perfect, including spiritual leaders. However, we must strive to be as whole as possible. Where weaknesses are found, accountable relationships will help to bolster and sustain through prayer and friendship. By searching God's Word and perseverance, God will take our weaknesses and make us strong, helping us to become leaders that will glorify God.

THE CALL TO SERVANTHOOD

Jesus said in Matthew 16:18:

> *"I also say to you that you are Peter, and upon this rock I will build My church; and the gates of Hades will not overpower it."*

Jesus is our supreme example of a true servant leader. He came to serve in life and death. During Christ's ministry His focus was on training His disciples to follow Him, as He followed His Father. He gave them ample opportunity to minister freely as they had received, (Matthew 10:8) and they matured into the full measure of their gifting and calling after the Holy Spirit was poured out on the Day of Pentecost.

In our modern times, the emphasis has shifted from His Church and our ministry to my church and my ministry. It is our hope and expectation that the Lord will bless our efforts. Rather than perceiving ourselves and acting as servants of the King of Kings, many leaders desire to be catered to. It has been said that the best "jobs" in the ghetto are the pimp, the pusher, the politician, the police, and the preacher. The reason for this belief is that all of these are people of power; a potential way out of a problematic, sometimes hopeless (at least perceived) situation. How tragic it is for many in urban centers or in our rural mega-churches that the perception of the preacher is that of an exploiter, not a servant willing to lay down his/her life for the sheep.

Biblically, no ministry is exclusive of the other. Therefore, to look at our calling without considering other callings in the Body of Christ is at best incomplete. Is it possible that the Church today is still wrestling with the question the disciples asked:

> *"Who then is greatest in the kingdom of heaven?"* (Matthew 18:1)

> *"But the greatest among you shall be your servant. Whoever exalts himself shall be humbled; and whoever humbles himself shall be exalted,"* (Matthew 23:11-12).

Jesus taught that the marks of greatness were humility and servanthood, not self-exaltation and promotion. There is no question that the Lord has provided for the victory of His Church and the exaltation of His Name in the earth. The question we must ask today is by what means has the Lord advocated in His Word to accomplish that goal?

In as much as Christ is our example of true servanthood, we must look to Him first to see the type of person we are to be.

WHY A SERVANT?

The whole world expected the Christ, the anointed one, to come in the form of a king. Instead, He came in the form of a servant:

> *"Let this mind be in you which was also in Christ Jesus, Who, being in the form of God, did not consider it robbery to be equal with God, but made himself of no reputation, taking on the form of a servant, and coming in the likeness of men. And being found in appearance as a man, he humbled himself and became obedient to the point of death, even the death of the cross"* (Philippians 2:5-8).

Jesus did not come as a king, to an exalted position in

the world system, or to the Jewish hierarchy, although He could have. He came in the most humble of states, as a commoner, seemingly no different than any other person in the land. He humbled Himself from His rightful position as God and became an obedient servant. Jesus became a servant, because it was His Father's will to win back His progeny, not through the commanding position of the throne, but through the lowly position of a servant.

We must accept from His model of life and the mandate of the Scriptures that we as the Body of Christ are to follow His example and, from the humility and servanthood of our lives, WIN A WORLD FOR JESUS.

JESUS SERVED HIS DISCIPLES

Jesus called and taught his disciples from the position of a servant. In John 13:1-20, Jesus serves His disciples. In an act of true humility, He washes their feet, as He guided, guarded and governed them. He counseled, exhorted and rebuked them as well in His training of His rag tag band. Through His love, they became all that God had intended them to be before the foundation of the earth. He is still doing that today in thousands of servant leaders world wide.

JESUS WAS EXALTED

"Therefore God exalted him to the highest place and gave him the name that is above every name, that at the name of Jesus every knee should bow, in heaven and on earth and under the earth, and every tongue confess that Jesus Christ is Lord, to the glory of God the Father" (Philippians 2:9-11).

The Lord was exalted beyond measure, because He was

the servant of all.

From God's perspective, one who is willing to lay down his life for his brothers and sisters is the only one deserving of exaltation.

THE PRESENT DAY SERVICE OF JESUS:

> *"But he, because he continues forever, has an unchangeable priesthood. Therefore, he is also able to save to the uttermost those who come to God through him, since he ever lives to make intercession for them"* (Hebrews 7:24).

When Jesus ascended on high and was seated in heavenly places, His life of earthly service was finished. But, His life of service took on another dynamic that operates to this day in the Church.

Jesus is in intense intercessory prayer for His Church. He is still praying the prayers of John 17, that we would hold to the Word of God, that we would keep His commandments and abide in His love. He is praying that we would learn to lay down our lives for one another, seeking unity in the Body of Christ.

Jesus is serving the Church through His prayers, to make us all that we can be so that He might reveal us to the world as the glorious church without spot or wrinkle (Ephesians 5:27).

We are the Body of Christ. As such, we are to be united, thus avoiding the indictment presented by the Apostle Paul in 1 Corinthians 1:10-13 which states;

> *"Now I exhort you, brethren, by the name of our Lord Jesus Christ, that you all agree, and there be no divisions among you, but you be made*

complete in the same mind and in the same judgment. Now I mean this, that each one of you is saying, 'I am of Paul,' and 'I of Apollos,' and 'I of Cephas,' and 'I of Christ.' Has Christ been divided? Paul was not crucified for you, was he? Or were you baptized in the name of Paul?"

Jesus Rejected The Exaltation Of Man By The Devil

"Again, the devil took him to a very high mountain and showed him the kingdoms of the world and their splendour. 'All this I will give you,' he said, 'if you will bow down and worship me.' Jesus said to him, 'Away from me, Satan!' For it is written: 'Worship the Lord your God, and serve him only,'" (Matthew 4:8-10).

Here we read Matthew's account of the third temptation of Jesus by Satan. The devil showed Jesus all the kingdoms of the earth and in essence said, "I'll make you the most powerful man on the face of the earth if you worship me." Jesus' answer showed His obedient, servant attitude and reinforced His great commitment to His Father. It is also notable that the disciples themselves, moved by the spirit of this world, tried to encourage Jesus to exalt Himself against the will of the Father.

"From that time on Jesus began to explain to his disciples that he must go to Jerusalem and suffer many things at the hands of the elders, chief priests and teachers of the law, and that he must be killed and on the third day be raised to life. Peter took him aside and began to rebuke him. 'Never, Lord!' he said. 'This shall never happen to you!' Jesus turned and said to Peter, 'Out of my sight,

Satan! You are a stumbling block to me; you do not have in mind the things of God, but the things of men'" (Matthew 16:21-23).

"When Jesus' followers saw what was going to happen, they said, 'Lord, should we strike with our swords?' And one of them struck the servant of the high priest, cutting off his right ear. But Jesus answered, 'No more of this!'" (Luke 22:49-51).

The spirit of the world encourages the sons of God to exalt themselves. The Spirit of Christ always speaks to the sons of men to humble themselves.

PAUL: EXAMPLE OF HUMILITY EXPRESSED:

Paul expressed humility in many sections of Scripture. Here are but three of the most poignant.

"For I am the least of the apostles and do not even deserve to be called an apostle, because I persecuted the church of God. But by the grace of God I am what I am, and his grace to me was not without effect" (1 Corinthians 15:9).

"Although I am less than the least of all God's people, this grace was given to me; to preach to the Gentiles..." (Ephesians 3:8).

"Do not cause anyone to stumble, whether Jews, Greeks or the church of God, even as I try to please everybody in every way. For I am not seeking my own good, but the good of many, so that they may be saved. Follow my example, as I follow the example of Christ" (1 Corinthians 10:32).

Paul had built in checks and balances in his relationship

with the Lord. He was well aware of his previous reprobate condition. The memory of his past kept him in check and facilitated his life as a servant. His work was the work of grace, the undeserved favor of the Lord.

Whenever someone loses sight of their beginnings, hearing and responding to the voice of the crowd to exalt himself, a fall is soon to follow.

Paul the Apostle, like so many of the great saints of God throughout Church history, understood that to conserve one's life or self leads to death, but to spend one's self for Christ and His Church is life. We need to return to His humble and appropriate perspective.

THE CALLING OF THE SAINTS

The saints of God are all called to walk in intimate fellowship with the Lord and one another. Leaders are to set the example of this godly life.

> *"...that all of them may be one, Father, just as you are in me and I am in you..."* (John 17:21a). *"There are different kinds of gifts, but the same Spirit. There are different kinds of service, but the same Lord. There are different kinds of working, but the same God works all of them in all men"* (1 Corinthians 12:4-6).

> *"As it is, there are many parts but one body. The eye cannot say to the hand, 'I don't need you!'And the head cannot say to the feet, 'I don't need you!' On the contrary, those parts of the body that seem to be weaker are indispensable"* (1 Corinthians 12:20-22).

> *"If the whole body were an eye, where would*

the sense of hearing be? If the whole body were an ear, where would the sense of smell be? But in fact God has arranged the parts in the body, every one of them, just as he wanted them to be" (1 Corinthians 12:17-18).

The exhortation of Jesus as well as Paul makes it abundantly clear that the members of the Body are mutually dependent upon one another for the Church to function properly. Whenever one member begins to work independent of another, a palsied condition arises and the whole Body ceases to function correctly.

"If one part suffers, every part suffers with it..." (1 Corinthians 12:26).

Once again, it is necessary for us to refer to the words of the Apostle Paul:

"Let this mind be in you which was also in Christ Jesus..." (Philippians 2:5)

Thus, the highest calling of the Saints is to serve. Our greatest calling on this earth is to love and serve the Lord our God with all of our being; our next priority is to love and serve one another.

The 60's were such turbulent times, with intense social upheaval. This led to the 70's and 80's with the focus on self-satisfaction, self-actualization, and self-abuse. The Church has been severely impacted negatively, by the spirit of the age, resulting in self-centered action by ministers and spiritual leaders. Could it be that the admonition of the Lord could relate to the self-absorbed minister of today? Let the Scripture provide for us sober thought:

"When the Son of man shall come in his glory,

and all the holy angels with him, then shall he sit upon the throne of his glory. And before him shall be gathered all nations: and he shall separate them one from another as a shepherd divideth his sheep from the goats: And he shall set the sheep on his right hand, but the goats on the left. Then shall the King say unto them on his right hand,' Come, ye blessed of my Father, inherit the kingdom prepared for you from the foundation of the world: For I was an hungered, and ye gave me meat: I was thirsty and ye gave me drink: I was a stranger, and ye took me in: Naked, and ye clothed me: I was sick, and ye visited me: I was in prison, and ye came unto me. Then shall the righteous answer him, Lord, when saw we thee an hungered, and fed thee? or thirsty and gave thee drink? When saw we thee a stranger, and took thee in? or naked and clothed thee? Or when saw we thee sick, or in prison, and came unto thee? And the King shall answer and say unto them, Verily I say unto you, Inasmuch as we have done it unto one of the least of these my brethren, ye have done it unto me. Then shall he say also unto them on the left hand, Depart from me, ye cursed, into everlasting fire, prepared for the devil and his angels. For I was an hungered, and ye gave me no meat: I was thirsty, and ye gave me no drink: I was a stranger, and ye took me not in: naked, and ye clothed me not: sick, and in prison and ye visited me not. Then shall they also answer him, saying, Lord, when saw we thee an hungered, or athirst, or a stranger, or naked, or sick, or in prison, and did not minister unto thee? Then shall he answer them, saying, Verily I say unto you, Inasmuch as ye did it not to one of the least of these, ye did it not to me. And these shall go away into everlasting punishment: but the righteous into life eternal." (Matthew 25:31-46, KJV)

"It is not fair to ask of others what you are unwilling to do yourself." Anna Eleanor Roosevelt

"Leadership is a combination of strategy and character. If you must be without one, be without the strategy."
Gen. H. Norman Schwarzkopf

"It may make a difference to all eternity whether we do right or wrong today." James Freeman Clark

CHAPTER 5

A CALL TO ACCOUNTABILITY:

I AM MY BROTHER'S KEEPER!

INTRODUCTION

I recently was in conversation with my friend and colleague, Dr. Randy Gurley on the state of the Church in the city. Dr. Gurley is in a unique position to observe the Church, as a resident of New York City and now a pastor outside Washington D.C. and a respected teacher in churches of all ethnic backgrounds. Our observation is that more than anything the Church needs to return to the basic premise that we must become accountable in love to one another. The Church in the city is fragmented, with pastors doing their own thing, following their own agenda. This is one of the primary strategies of the devil; to divide and conquer the Church. A call to biblical unity is being heard around the world, a unity based upon mutual respect and honest accountability which leads to corporate (church) integrity.

AM I MY BROTHER'S KEEPER?

"Then the Lord said to Cain, 'Where is Abel your brother?' And he said, 'I do not know. Am I my brother's keeper?'" (Genesis 4:9).

Throughout the ages the hearts of men have been asking this question. In a world that advocates each man for himself, it is difficult to know the answer. Not until the coming of the Lord Jesus did we gain a clear view of the truth of this issue. He answered beyond a shadow of doubt that we are our brother's keeper.

> "They devoted themselves to the apostles' teaching and to the fellowship, to the breaking of bread, and to prayer. Everyone was filled with awe, and many wonders and miraculous signs were done by the apostles. All the believers were together and had everything in common. Selling their possessions and goods, they gave to anyone as he had need. Every day they continued to meet together in the temple courts. They broke bread in their homes and ate together with glad and sincere hearts, praising God and enjoying the favor of all the people. And the Lord added to their number daily those who were being saved" (Acts 2:42-47).

This is a model of life that the Holy Spirit laid out for His people to follow forever.

> "Anyone who claims to be in the light but hates his brother is still in the darkness. Whoever loves his brother lives in the light, and there is nothing in him to make him stumble. But whoever hates his brother is in the darkness and walks around in the darkness; he does not know where he is going, because the darkness has blinded him" (1 John 2:9-11).

A lack of love in practical terms for the brethren brings into question our very salvation. The word "brother" in the Greek is the word *adelphos*. This denotes fellowship among people from similar origin; members meeting one another's needs and sharing the love of Jesus with all who receive Him. We must have the same love for the Christian community. 1 John 2:10-11 states that he who loves his brother abides in the light, and there is no cause for stumbling in Him. Esteeming the brethren is not a matter of choice, but a command from the Lord.

> *"Therefore if there is any consolation in Christ, if any comfort of love, if any fellowship of the Spirit, if any affection and mercy, fulfill my joy by being like minded, having the same love, being of one accord, of one mind. Let nothing be done through selfish ambition and conceit, but in lowliness of mind let each esteem others better than himself. Let each of you look not only for his own interests, but also for the interests of others"* (Philippians 2:1-4).

Our care for the brethren is the measure and the mark of our greatness.

ACCOUNTABILITY AND TEAM MINISTRY

When Jesus called the disciples, He specifically called them as a **team**. He called twelve, gathered them around Him for three years and taught them, among other things, the value of team ministry and accountability. Though the process of creating this team must have been a life with internal conflict and strife (such as bickering over position), they were indeed molded as a team.

Together they were taught the Kingdom of God by the words and works of Jesus. Together they were corrected and rebuked. Together they were sensitized to the things of the Spirit. Together they were taught the power of God's Word. Not one of them was greater or lesser than the other, for we know God is no respecter of persons. The only difference between them, other than their personality traits, was their gifts and callings. Each of them learned to respect the other in his particular arena of anointing, realizing that he was incomplete without the other. They always had multiplied ability among them, providing protection from Satan's inroads into their lives.

Only one of the original twelve disciples went into darkness – Judas. We must ask ourselves why? One possible explanation is that he never subjected himself to the scrutiny of his brothers. There were hidden agendas in his heart that he refused to deal with, resulting in an immoral, dishonest lifestyle.

Judas' life was secretive. He presents from scripture as aloof and detached which served to ultimately destroy him. This destructive lifestyle brings the same result in today's church.

Jesus never used a rod to illustrate how we would bring men into the Kingdom of God, He used a net. Nets take the help of the whole to bring in the harvest. One man alone could only bring in a few fish in a net, but many working together can bring in multitudes of fish. It is time for the Church to wake up to the fact that when we operate as God intended, in cooperative effort, there will be ever greater harvest than previously seen.

EXAMPLE "OF THE BAPTIST"

John the Baptist was a mighty prophet of God who preached the Kingdom of God in the spirit of Elijah. So powerful was his ministry and so pure was his life, that Jesus commended him as the greatest man born from women.

When John first ministered, the crowds would come. But, when Jesus began to minister, even his disciples began to follow after the "new leader on the block."

John's response to Christ's popularity is interesting, especially in light of frequent leaders' reports today. His statement was that Jesus must increase, but I must decrease (John 3). As difficult as this may have been for John, he recognized who he was and who he wasn't. He came to focus men to Christ, not to himself. His joy was complete knowing that the bridegroom was come, bringing salvation to the world. He willingly stepped aside for the greater ministry, and will be honored forever for his humility and ministry. God has called us to be fellow workers for the Gospel.

Once the foundation of brotherhood has truly laid, there is nothing that leaders cannot do together. Great apostles, prophets, evangelists, pastors, and teachers can all do what they are good at and at the same time reap the benefits from other gifts.

Before Jesus commissioned the disciples to their ministries, He taught them humility and servanthood through their accountable relationships with one another. Further, He taught them the epitome of working together. In Matthew 10, Jesus sends the disciples out, giving them power over sickness, disease, and unclean spirits. He told them to preach the gospel of the kingdom. They labored together as a team in the proclamation of the gospel. We also see them working together in feeding the five thousand (Luke 9). Note that these men were all apostles, each submitted to the other. We must not be afraid to work with leaders of the same or greater giftings than ourselves. The blessings will be tremendous.

The responsibility of the Church is too great for one person to handle and the decisions will soon wear down the most tenacious of men working as a team. This eliminates the frustration of the pastor who cannot win souls, but has a vision for many. He can move alongside the evangelist working as a team and see the vision accomplished. This eliminates the frustration of the evangelist who can win souls but cannot disciple them. Through the pastor, he can see thousands won to Christ and brought into the fullness of Jesus. Oh, the joy of being able to concentrate your efforts on the things that God has called you to and still enjoy the fruit of what you are not called to do.

WE ARE FELLOW SOLDIERS OF THE CROSS

Paul and Silas are probably the greatest New Testament examples of brothers fighting together. As they did the work of the Lord, they were committed to prison, being frequently beaten as a reward. Most men would have given up, but not them. They encouraged one another in the Lord and found Jesus in every circumstance they encountered. Paul said he had learned in every circumstance to be content.

> *"I know what it is to be in need, and I know what it is to have plenty. I have learned the secret of being content in any and every situation, whether well-fed or hungry, whether living in plenty or in want. I can do everything through him who gives me strength,"* (Philippians 4:12-13).

How many men are there today, who are carrying burdens, the Lord never intended them to carry? How many men and women of God are ministering alone, bearing little fruit, but inside are fighting overwhelming odds against various temptations. Peter's greatest fall came when he separated himself from the brethren, ending in the denial of his Lord. It is time for men and women to shun the desire to surround ourselves with only those submitted to us and join forces with men and women of like passion and vision. Together, multiple visions can be fulfilled, which at this moment seem unreachable.

Whenever there is a move amongst leaders of God to unite in team ministry, with mutual accountability, hell will fight with a vengeance. Darkness hates light, but will tolerate small lights shining alone. However, when small lights begin to cluster together, especially in prayer, believing for the fresh breath of God to blow on their lights, thus expanding and intensifying the glow, the devil will attempt to sabotage. All he has to use is deception, but he will use it any way he can, with an onslaught of temptation. (Since his utter defeat by Christ on the cross, his only real power). The lust of the flesh will be intensified, the lust of the eyes will attack and especially the pride of life will rear its ugly head. The focus is to bring the wants out of each of us, thus a committed relationship of mutual accountability, love and respect is needed to withstand the devil's schemes. United we stand, divided we fall. May the Lord give us wisdom to unite in heart and purpose for the greater good of the Body of Christ.

"I submit to you that if a man hasn't discovered something he will die for, he isn't fit to live." Martin Luther King, Jr.

"A sensible man watches for problems ahead and prepares to meet them. The simpleton never looks, and suffers the consequences." Proverbs 27:12

"A man has made at least a start on discovering the meaning of human life when he plants shade trees under which he knows full well he will never sit." D. Elton Trueblood

CHAPTER 6

THE LIFE OF A LEADER

INTRODUCTION

All leaders, whether in the inner city or the most rural setting, need to prepare themselves for the long haul. The race we run is an endurance race, not a sprint (Hebrews 12:2). Thus, how we live in practical terms is nearly as important as our internal preparation of character, knowledge, understanding and wisdom. Although this section does comprehensively address areas of the maturing/enduring process and prayers, it highlights the most important to ensure process in ministry leadership development.

THE LEADER'S WALK

The leader is a whole person, needing to cultivate his total self. Thus, the leader must train his body, as well as his mind and spirit.

TRAIN YOUR BODY

Our body is the temple of the Holy Spirit. We are admonished to treat it with respect. Our model is not Sylvester Stallone, but we should do all we can to stay in shape. Good diet, health, exercise, adequate rest, positive relationships, and managing our stress are all components of a healthy temple. It is an important part of our ministerial effectiveness and longevity.

As ministers, there can be personal habits and mannerisms that can negatively affect our work. Awareness of ourselves is a worthy goal. However, our awareness must not become preoccupation. The body we have is all we have, so you might as well accept that we must practice a relaxed but steady control of bodily movements. Constant fidgeting, shifting, and scratching are not only signs of "nerves," but often just plain old bad habits.

In ministry we need to show self-control with our hands. Learn to keep them still. Don't allow your hands to tyrannize you by constant, restless motion. Shake hands firmly and warmly, then let go courteously and positively.

Ministers need good posture. Shuffling feet and a habitual slouch give people the vague, uneasy feeling that your mind shuffles and slouches too. An outward alertness in stance and carriage not only conveys a better impression but tends to create the feeling of life within yourself.

Watch your eyes. Practice looking at the same person to whom you are speaking or listening. Avoid the habit of gazing around as though bored; give the person in front of you your complete attention, as if no one else mattered at that moment.

One of the problems that all leaders face is time management. Leaders must **CULTIVATE PUNCTUALITY**.

"Not slothful in business; fervent in spirit; serving the Lord" (Romans 12:11). Make yourself be punctual. The habit of being on time will never be acquired unless you are convinced that Christian courtesy demands it and you plan ahead, so that you know where you need to be and when.

Keep a daily reminder of all appointments. Look ahead, and start early. John Wesley said, "I am always in haste but never in a hurry." He meant that though he had no time for idleness, he allowed himself sufficient time to carry out his undertakings calmly and punctually.

Christian leaders are admonished to **"GIRD UP" YOUR MIND.**

Therefore, prepare your minds for action..." (1 Peter 1:13). God's work demands trained minds. Peter's command to "gird up the loins of your mind" uses the picture of a man in New Testament times gathering up his loose robes with a girdle when in a hurry or starting on a journey. In the same way, gather up your mind, organize the loose ends, control your wandering thoughts.

In the New Testament, all the saved ones are priests; therefore all the saved ones should serve, only when all are serving is the Church strong (1 Corinthians 12:14-19, 28-30).

Part of girding up your mind is learning perspective in the Body of Christ. We must pay special attention to the Body. Not everyone receives the same measure of grace. Since the grace that each receives varies, the gifts received by each before God also vary (Romans 12:3, 6).

Those who serve must concentrate on their service (Romans 12:6-21). Everyone who is gifted, be it in the ministry of the Word, or of serving others, the command is that we serve according to our grace. Thus, we do not interfere with others' affairs and step on others' feet. Walk your way and act according to the gift given to you by God. If you prophesy, prophesy according to your gifts and measure of faith. He that exhorts, let him exhort without trying to interfere with others. He that rules, let him rule properly in the Church and not lord it over others.

We all have certain talents, and are to use them for God's glory. Regardless whether you are a ten, five, two or one talent person, you are required by the Lord to use your talent to the best of your ability for the Master.

Even though you may have received but one talent, you still must use it. 1 Corinthians 12:22-25 says,

> *"No, much rather, those members of the body which seem to be weaker are necessary. And those members of the body which we think to be less honorable, on these we bestow greater honor; and our unpresentable parts have greater modesty, but our presentable parts have no need. But God composed the body, having given greater honor to that part which lacks it, that there should be no schism in the body, but that the members should have the same care for one another."*

God gives the resources of His Kingdom for us to take and multiply, *"to every man according to his several abilities"* (Matthew 25:15. See 1 Corinthians 12:18).

If someone who will not serve, but buries his talent, the Church suffers. If there are members who are not functioning, it will cause the Body to suffer (1 Corinthians 12:26). When one member "withholds" from the church, the Body of Christ "results" in poverty (Proverbs 11:24).

When a talent is buried, God takes the one talent from that member and gives it to the member who is functioning fruitfully. The member who is left with nothing is unprofitable (Matthew 25:24-30).

What does the one-talent member do? Either attempt to work alone, often from dawn to dusk, which leaves others idle and the church unproductive.

A leader is busy from morning to evening causing all the one-talent ones to work, this is the Church serving, this is the Church preaching the Gospel. This is the right principle

– body life in operation (Matthew 25:34-40). Body life includes:

- Giving meat to the hungry
- Giving drink to the thirsty
- Ministering to strangers
- Visiting the sick
- Ministering to the destitute
- Going to those in prison
- Giving
- Being hospitable
- Showing mercy (Luke 10:36-37)

Body life, the church in action, is a primary result of effective leadership. There are also many other opportunities for serving the Body, such as music, singing, cleaning, praying, exhorting, etc. The key is to cultivate these talents and direct them for the blessing of the Church, and fulfill the work of God.

THE LEADER'S TALK

Most of the readers of this text are presently Bible College students, or lay leaders desiring increased understanding "of their role" as leader. If, however, you are already a leader with years of hermeneutical training behind you, you may want to merely skim this section as a reminder of your previous learning.

There is no substitute in the leader's life for prayer and studying the Word. Let's look at the requirements for studying the Word of God (2 Timothy 3:14-17).

First, there must be a **sincere desire for the Word** (1 Peter 2:1-2). This desire is a heart desire, to know the Lord in greater measure through His Word. However, even if the desire to study is not evident, we must have a **willingness to study out of obedience to** God's Word. We do this through study even when we don't care to. Our study means **searching the Scriptures** (Acts 17:11-12), to determine the meaning in the message of the Word and to receive **revelation of the Holy Spirit** (1 Corinthians 2:9-16) to share with His church.

The illumination of the mind by the Holy Spirit allows us to comprehend truth and thus relate it to the congregation. We should also be willing to submit to the anointed **instruction by teachers** (1 Corinthians 12:28) *"And God has set some in the church, first apostles, secondarily prophets, thirdly teachers..."* God has set the extension of His Son in the earth in human vessels who are anointed by Him to impart truth and instruct in His ways to become mature, full grown as His Body.

With our study and receiving of instruction comes an increase in our **ability to understand** (John 8:43). This is an ability which necessitates hearing. This hearing is receiving the truth, and is conditional on a right relationship with God.

So, how should we study? It is strongly recommended that one **read the whole Bible consecutively**. As you read, it is recommended that you ask yourself the following questions on each chapter and write them down in a notebook.[8]

1. What is the main subject of this chapter (in a single sentence)?
2. Who are the main persons in this chapter?

---

[8] For more on this see *Fresh Manna: Introduction to the Study of God's Word*, by Dr. DeKoven

3. What truth is most emphasized?
4. What lessons do I receive?
5. What is the key verse?
6. What does it teach about Christ?

Secondly, write an **outline study of each book of the Bible**. Conduct a summary of the book, key verse, author, time covered, and central theme. This has been done by many writers in books on Bible survey. However, nothing substitutes for your personal work, and the excitement of receiving fresh revelation from the Lord as you do so.

Before we understand how the Bible applies to the Church, we should know how it applies to Christ in types, shadows and symbols. Thus, a study of Christ in Scripture, found in each book, is an outstanding method for personal growth.

Character Studies of men and women in the Bible can reveal much. Many truths and principles are hidden in Bible characters such as Enoch, David, Abraham, Saul, Ruth, Peter and Paul.

Word Studies. Take a word and go through the Bible on it, e.g., suddenly, steadfast, now, violent, fight, midnight, the door.

We should also know how to do **subject or topical studies**. Look up the following subjects and follow them through in your concordance: Holy Ghost, God, faith, water baptism, hell, heaven, praise, salvation, healing.

Chapter studies are also recommended. Dissect a chapter, such as Psalm 23 or another dynamic chapter. Many important themes can be found in the rich forum of study.

Finally, become aware of **name meanings**. Find out the

meaning of a person, city, tribe, tree, river, and mountain. Example: Judah means praise. In Numbers 2:3, Judah led in the marching of the camps.

Most of these study skills have been or should have been learned in your Bible College or Seminary education if you had the opportunity to attend one. If not, there are several recommended books, which are listed in the Bibliography, which can assist you.

How Is The Christian Leader To Study?

First, be a specialist.

Every Christian worker should be a specialist in the Word of God. It is our foundation, guide, and authority.

To study well, we must be prepared to work. It is real work to study the Bible. The Bereans searched the Scriptures (Acts 17:11). Paul says we are to be diligent in dividing the Word of truth (2 Timothy 2:15). The Word is like a mine, most great truths do not lie upon the surface. They need to be 'mined' and that means patient labor. Thus, you must set aside sufficient time to study God's Word.

Remember, the devil opposes the Word and those who make a genuine study of it, and he will seek to fill our time with irrelevant things to distract us from consistently studying the Word. Discipline and much determination are vital to daily Bible Study, therefore we must study the Word daily and consistently (Acts 17:11). You should set a time every day – the morning may be the best time for some, the evening for others.

In either case, study when your faculties are keenest and when you have the greatest privacy and quiet.

You must study **prayerfully** (Psalm 119:18). Prayer will

open your eyes to vital truths in the Word. The Holy Spirit is the greatest interpreter of the Word (John 16:12-13). He comes in answer to prayer, or to reveal truth to us to share with others.

Recognize the Bible as the Word of God. Believe everything in the Bible according to good rules of evangelical hermeneutics, with one all-important desire — to know the mind of God (1 Thessalonians 2:13).

In our study, we should **appropriate the Word**. The Bible should be studied as eagerly as a hungry man seeks for bread. The formal reading of a portion of Scripture each day may have some real value as a religious exercise, but in order that the full benefit may be received from its truths, they must be appropriated to personal needs. If it says "we are more than conquerors," apply it, appropriate it, thank Him for it, confess it.

It is helpful to **meditate on the Word**. Follow your Bible study with meditation, that is, think about what you have read. Ponder, muse, reflect on the things of God (Psalm 1:1-2; 19:14; 119:15, 23, 48, 97, 148.)

I always recommend note taking during daily study. By using a small notebook or the margin of your Bible, thoughts are clarified, new questions for further study form, providing a record of how God has spoken to you day by day, and also helps refresh your memory concerning things that the Holy Spirit speaks to you.

Don't be afraid to **mark your Bible**. As you do so, the Bible becomes doubly precious to the owner and preserves the result of years of study. It keeps outstanding truths fresh before the mind. Select themes and mark them consecutively.

The receiving of revelation of the Word, through study, is not receiving a blinding flash of God's ways and purposes or some other dramatic experience. It means that by your study, you have "uncovered" a truth hidden in the Word, one that others may also have "uncovered" or had revealed to them long ago.

It has been said that the two best tools for effective sermon preparation are the Bible and the daily newspaper. Preaching should be relevant to **circumstances and need**. Any need or circumstance that is apparent should provoke you to thought for a sermon or teaching on this subject.

Example: If many are in need of salvation, the Holy Spirit, etc., then this should be sufficient to prompt you to a message that will meet the need. If the congregation is spiritually lethargic, this could prompt a message against lukewarmness, or sacrifice of praise, faith, trials, etc.

Be prepared to receive **direct inspiration**. Perhaps on a walk, a drive, during a praise service, or anywhere else you might receive a sudden inspiration, then pursue it and develop the thought. I call my morning shower my "shower of power," as I often receive fresh thoughts from the Lord as the water cascades against me.

The cry of your own heart is the best message you can present. After we have allowed God to deal with us personally, through various experiences, we can minister more effectively to others.

Much of our leadership is measured by the message we present, both content and delivery. Thus, you must find the message God wants for the time. You become his mouthpiece (Exodus 4:11-12; Proverbs 22:17-21). Wait on the Lord and let Him direct you.

At all times, have an aim. Be able to express your aim or theme in one short sentence once you know what God wants you to preach.

Collect your material by using a concordance or cross-reference. Listen to other preachers, read other sermons and write down things that are quickened to you; these can give seed thoughts that can be developed for your actual message.

Relating the text to present day life is a necessary art form.

Study the text minutely. Find the meaning of the words and phrases used. Also, study the text in immediate connection with the context of the Scripture.

Compare various translations and versions, using a Concordance and a Bible dictionary to ensure further clarity.

Prayerfully determine how this can be applied to those you are going to speak to. What does God want emphasized?

When it is time to present the "Thus saith the Lord" to the congregation, **have a plan**. It is amazing to me how charismatic preachers (especially) will approach the pulpit unprepared, expecting God to give them a "word" as they open their mouth. There is no substitute for preparation before preaching and teaching, recognizing that the Holy Spirit moves best through order, not chaos.

For review purposes, a simple outline of a sermon includes the **introduction**. This prepares the minds of hearers with opening remarks to get their attention (and hopefully keep it!).

Use general knowledge possessed by the hearers to

introduce your topics. Often current events are helpful for illustration. Use a striking point to gain their ear. If you awaken expectation and give the aim of your message, you are more likely to gain the ear of your audience.

Don't be afraid to let the Holy Spirit lead in other directions other than your prepared notes, you can always come back to them later. However, this should be rare. Also, **illustrations** are used to throw light on the truth you are presenting.

Remember your **conclusion**. Formulate in a few sentences what you are aiming for. You want to leave your congregation with a truth that has **application**. Apply the message to them, how they may experience that truth. A practical sermon is usually the best received.

Count on the **anointing**. The Holy Spirit transforms lives, not through manipulations of emotions and use of tricks to motivate them but through prepared and spirit-filled preaching of the Word of life.

Let me close with some helpful thoughts.

Be yourself...avoid imitating media celebrities. Preach and teach from a style that fits you best.

Don't apologize for what is to be said, if it is God's Word.

Encourage people, but don't drive them. You can lead a horse to water, but you can't make him drink. However, good preaching/teaching will pour salt in their oats.

Have a burden for the people and your community. Many have written off the city as a lost cause, but the Lord hasn't. God is still in the business of transforming lives, families, cities and nations. Your burden expressed to the people will ignite their compassion for the community, as you sincerely express it in your ministry.

"The function of leadership is to produce more leaders, not more followers." Ralph Nadar

"A man who wants to lead the orchestra must turn his back on the crowd." Max Lucado

The key to successful leadership today is influence, not authority." Kenneth Blanchard

CHAPTER 7

A CALL TO SPIRITUAL LEADERSHIP

THE MINISTRY CALL

In Matthew 16:18 we read *"...I will build my Church and the gates of hell will not prevail against it."* The Church does not belong to man or organization, but to Christ. As leaders, we are merely stewards of what God has entrusted to us. Under Christ, the five-fold ministry has been given by Christ as gifts to the Church, and are all needed to equip the saints for works of service (Ephesians 4:10-13).

The most active and visible five-fold minister in the church is usually the pastor. As a leader chosen by the Lord, he/she is to work in unity with the other gifts, and in harmony as a chief amongst equals with the elders, deacons and other gifted members of Christ's Body.[9]

Pastoral leaders, especially those called to the city, must recognize the importance of their position in the Church, and the need to work in unity and harmony with the other gifts and ministry in the Body of Christ.

Psalm 23 reads, *"The Lord is my Shepherd"* (*Jehovah Raah*). Ultimately God the Father, and Jesus (the Good Shepherd), are the examples of the pastor in action and is to be the heart of all gift ministries (Apostle, Prophet, Evangelist, Teacher, Pastor).

Raah means "to feed" in Hebrew; the emphasis is

---

[9] Many disagree with elders as separate from pastors, as the term is virtually synonymous. For more see *Strategic Church Administration*.

on the ability to feed sheep. In the New Testament, the words "pastor" and "shepherd" are synonymous, indicating one who tends or herds flocks. Pastors guide as well as feed the flock. This involves tender care and vigilant oversight, with a focus on the welfare of those under care.

> **Acts 20:28**: *"Take heed...to FEED the church of God..."* **Jeremiah 3:15**: *"I will give you pastors...which shall FEED you with knowledge and understanding."* **John 21:15-16**: *"...FEED my lambs...FEED my sheep."*

The Greek word for pastor or shepherd is *poimaino* which means "to feed" and "to rule." Thus, the role of a pastor in the local church is to feed the precious sheep of God and lead them into righteousness.

Jesus is the type and example for every under-shepherd, pastor or spiritual leader.

In **John 10:11**, Jesus says of Himself, *"I am the good shepherd: the good shepherd giveth his life for the sheep."* Further, **John 10:14**: *"I am the good shepherd, and know my sheep and am known of mine."* Leaders stand in the stead of Jesus Christ to guard and feed His flock on earth. This is an awesome responsibility.

APOSTOLIC LEADERSHIP[10]

The simplest definition of an apostle is "a sent one." He/she is a gift, a part of the ministry of Christ sent to lay foundation for the ministry being built or the foundation of the revelation of Christ as Lord and King.

---

[10] Please forgive these all-to-brief summaries of these vital gifts to the body of Christ.

The message of the apostle (a function, not specifically an office) is the kingdom of God. God frequently uses the apostolic gift to establish churches and ministries in new areas, re-built and re-establish (set in order, Titus ____) existing churches, and establish the rule of Christ (Love God, love your neighbor) in believers.

Further, an apostle will diligently teach and train local leaders, eventually ordaining elders in locality, moving on through maintaining a relationship with the newly established work.

PROPHETIC LEADERSHIP

A prophet is a gift to the church at large, with specific anointing to see and declare God's intentions for a person, place, or ministry. This vital ministry, working with apostolic leadership, is the one-two punch of the foundation of the church. Further, the true prophetic gift actively teaches believers to hear the voice of God and prophecies the Spirit gives utterance.

EVANGELISTIC LEADERSHIP

The evangelistic gift to the church has the ability to win souls to Christ and inspire/equip others to do the same. Though little is found in scripture regarding the evangelist, it is nonetheless a vital component for the propagation of the gospel and the equipping of the saints for mature service.

THE PASTOR/TEACHER LEADER

These gifts, similar but with different emphasis are combined by many writers as one gift. However, having been part-teachers in action; "they" are truly a gift to the Body. Teachers impart from study of scripture, the Word of life in a dynamic like no other. Teachers are vital to the maturing of the Body, as are pastors.

OBSERVATIONS

In fact, all five spiritual gifts along with elders, deacons and ministries are supposed to work together. Sadly, this is rarely seen. However, it remains an ideal and a matter for prayer. Further, all gifts should in fact meet the criteria (character) of elder to be qualified to function as leaders for Christ's church.

THE CALL TO SPIRITUAL LEADERSHIP

The spiritual leader's calling is to the area of responsibility over which he is placed. He/she is willing to feed, to guard, and to lead God's people into the purposes of God. The pastor is a gift sent from God (Ephesians 4:11-13).

In order to become a pastor, a man must receive a call from God. Bible schools and seminaries have their place, but unless a man is commissioned and sent by God, theological education will scarcely equip him/her for ministry. Bible schools can often be sterile environments in which to grow. Without training in the local church, under a Spirit-filled, God-appointed leader who recognizes the call on a young Christian's life, proper direction and guidance is often neglected.

The ability to care for a flock or lead a ministry is strictly a gift from God; it is not learned in academic institutions, but through the life of the church itself. The ability to love people and dedicate one's life to their service, comes from the heart. God places this concern and care into the heart of a leader. Whoever God calls to lead a church or ministry is given an anointing and grace to feed, to guide, and to care for the people God has placed under him or her. Sometimes this is a thankless and tiresome responsibility, but because of the special gift of God, he/she loves and stays with the men and women they have been called to lead.

A LEADER'S RESPONSIBILITY - AN OVERSEER

The definition of oversight is to watch over, to look upon (tend sheep, and rule over are from the same root word):

> *"Obey them that have the rule over you, and submit yourselves; for they watch for your souls..."* (Hebrews 13:17) (to guard the souls of his flock).

Further, Jesus and Paul discuss some principles of oversight: *"But he that is greatest among you shall be your servant"* (Matthew 23:11). A servant's attitude is needed. This has already been covered in sufficient detail.

Luke 22:25-26: Jesus portrays the attitude for leaders to adopt.

1 Peter 5:3: *"Neither as being lords over God's heritage, but being examples to the flock."* We are to recognize our role as under-shepherds, not "lords."

Further, we are to guard and protect. The spiritual leader watches for the enemies of the sheep thieves, wolves, hirelings, and strangers. They defend the flock against intruders. These can include false any form of five-fold ministers. The leader sleeps by the door of the sheepfold. The porter is the Holy Spirit. Not everyone who wants to get into the fold is admitted. The fold is protected from those sheep having contagious spiritual diseases (rebellion). Also, a hireling works for the money – he/she doesn't care if a wolf comes to destroy the sheep, but leaves the flock the time of danger (John 10:12).

A leader's heart goes out to protect the weak, the fragile, the homeless and malnourished. They will strengthen those with weaknesses, personality flaws, emotional problems. He will steer ruined lives back to health (Ezekiel 34:1-15).

Another primary function of the whole five-fold ministry and elders is to teach. We are to impart knowledge which will lead to understanding and ultimately to wisdom:

> *"And the things that thou hast heard of me among many witnesses, the same commit thou to faithful men, who shall be able to teach others also"* (2 Timothy 2:2).

The leader sets the pace of the flock, leading by example.

A leader must know how to pace the flock. Sheep are led, not driven. If the young, weak, or weary need to rest, a leader will stop the whole flock for the one. The Lord follows a principle which is opposed to the world's philosophy of "survival of the fittest."

In Isaiah 40:11 we see that a good leader will carry those in need, those who can't make it on their own. Sometimes sheep will lie down and give up. Someone must carry them over the rough spots.

A personal relationship with the sheep is necessary to be an effective leader. The leader calls them by name (**personal relationship**) and leads them out to pasture (John 10:3).

The leader is willing to discipline the sheep. To discipline means to teach and to correct, to encourage soundness of mind and to practice godliness.

One stumbling block to the flock is the futile effort of

sheep trying to discipline sheep. Correction comes from the leader and elders; it is not a child's job to discipline his father's children. Finally, through discipline we reproduce other leaders. The law of God is that each reproduces after its kind. Shepherds are approved to train other shepherds, evangelists to train other evangelists, apostles to train other apostles, etc. (Genesis 1:11; Acts 20:28; 1 Timothy 5:21).

THE NATURE OF SHEEP IS TO BE LED

God's people are frequently compared to sheep in the Word of God. The characteristics of sheep include the fact that they are followers and are easily led:

"He...leadeth them out" (John 10:3).

"My sheep hear my voice, and I know them and they follow me" (John 10:27).

Secondly, they won't follow a stranger. They are trained to hear and trust one voice, and one voice only:

"And a stranger they simply will not follow, but will flee from him, because they do not know the voice of strangers" (John 10:5).

Sheep have a tendency to go astray (Isaiah 53:6; Psalm 119:67). They need constant surveillance. The primary function of a leader is to guide and lead his flock away from dangers and snares. Finally, sheep have many enemies and no natural defenses. Thus, they are helpless, with no sense of direction. The need for oversight is obvious. Often this does not mean sheep are mindless; all are priests and kings before the Lord. All can hear from God and must be respected.

RESPONSIBILITIES OF THE SHEEP TO THE SHEPHERD

The sheep have responsibilities to the leadership. They

include obedience, *"That you submit yourselves unto such, and to everyone that helpeth with us, and laboureth"* (1 Corinthians 16:16). A true sheep will relinquish his right to guide his own life to the leader under the guidance of the Holy Spirit, realizing that the leader is GOD'S CHOICE and GOD'S VOICE (of course, none is infallible).

Further, they will pray for the leadership of the church, trusting God to guide them:

"...For the love of the Spirit, that ye strive together with me in your prayers to God for me," (Romans 15:30) *"You also helping together by prayer for us..."* (2 Corinthians 1:11). Also, the sheep are not to receive an accusation against a minister:

> *"Against an elder receive not an accusation, but before two or three witnesses"* (1 Timothy 5:19).

Finally, the response of the flock to the leader, as unto Christ, is to hear and know his familiar voice and be willing to follow and obey him, and then they have rest and peace. They gladly acknowledge his leadership because it is the nature of a sheep to follow.

PSEUDO LEADERS

Unfortunately, there are many men and women who function out of their gifting or for wrong motivation. The Scriptures discuss them under the names of hirelings, thieves, robbers, wolves, goats, wheat and tares.

Hirelings represent ministers who don't personally care for the flock because they care only for themselves and their own gain.

They have no real authority. They are often subject to hiring and firing by church boards and administrations. On the contrary, the Scriptures portray a leader as a faithful servant of God and the people, who adheres to the flock no matter what the turmoil, distress, or danger. The practice of transferring pastors, especially from church to church, is absolutely contrary to biblical standards.

Thieves and robbers are "ministers" who do not enter in by the door (John 10:8-9). The door is Jesus who ordains and approves leaders. Any ministry that seeks to operate without the knowledge or the blessing of leadership is working under the "back door principle." They are usually out working in rebellion to ordained authority and ultimately are out to destroy the spiritual lives of innocent sheep, placing them under deception. Jesus emphasized that anyone who did not enter into the fold by the door is a thief and a destroyer.

The nature of the wolf is to stalk the prey and then to attack the ones who go astray:

> *"Some shall depart from the faith, giving heed*
> *to seducing spirits and doctrines of devils"*
> (Matthew 7;15; Acts 20:30; 1 Timothy 4:1).

The Holy Spirit sows only good seed and positive thoughts. No one could make a count of the number of Christians who have fallen prey to a ravening wolf. The protection of a Christian lies in the sheepfold, where he grazes contentedly with the flock. Any sheep who becomes discontent and strays away becomes prey to the predators of sheep. Wolves may come in the costume of a false prophet, a television evangelist, or a Christian celebrity with a new doctrine. True leaders watch for deception and protect their flock from harm.

The safeguard for the sheep is the Body of Christ. The

admonition to the sheep is, "Don't wander solitarily; always remain with the flock." The sheep must not reject a true shepherd's decision or refuse to follow the True Shepherd. No leader is perfect, but those who are called and placed deserve support and loyalty.

Goats graze with sheep, but have a completely different nature. They will not follow and must be driven. They are often troublemakers in the flock, causing contention, taking food, arguing, they are never happy. At the final judgment, Jesus will separate the goats from the sheep (Matthew 25:32).

In conclusion, it is God's purpose to unite every born-again believer to a **local church fellowship**. It is in the confines of the flock that God gives the spiritual leader as a precious and needful gift to the Body (individually and jointly). The sheep, without anointed leadership, will soon fall prey to the many wiles and strategies of the devil, of whom it is said "...he goes about like a roaring lion, seeking whom he may devour" (1 Peter 5:8). It is not burdensome to submit to such leadership, knowing that therein lies the safety, nourishment, and protection of the sheepfold.

The pastor is responsible for much of the care of the flock. He/she must be well trained and prepared to meet the endless demands which will be made on his/her life. They must be tested, tried, and be found true, that they will not flee when danger or upheavals arise. They must be well-seasoned, well prepared, **and willing to serve the people they lead**. The spiritual leader is a gift from God Himself - to stand in His stead to love, to care for, to feed, and to tend the sheep for whom Christ gave His life.

LOCAL CHURCH LEADERSHIP

As we have seen from the emerging scriptural pattern,

God has determined that the local church should be governed by especially anointed persons serving in the callings of the five-fold ministry. Generally these persons are called elders in scripture, referring to the wisdom and ability necessary to hold such an office.

Due to the nature of the position of elder, God has required specific spiritual, character, domestic, and ministry qualifications of persons being considered for eldership. These have been specified in 1 Timothy 3 and Titus 1.

ROLE OF ELDERSHIP

Recent developments in the Church indicate that it is more important than ever for believers to properly understand the role of elders. As instruments of God's government, New Testament elders are called to administer the love and discipline of God which keep His people within the boundaries of protection and safety.

The term, "elder," is translated from the Greek, *presbuteron*, and literally means "old men." The term has been used in Jewish society to refer to the group of leaders having governmental oversight of the nation and individual cities. Historically, elders sat in the gates of the cities to watch the coming and goings of the people. They were there to watch for danger approaching and to sound the alarm when it did. Governmental actions were carried out when the elders sat in the gates. Scripture gives a clear description of the overall job of five-fold ministry and elders in the Church.

Responsibilities include:

- Prayer and intercession (Acts 6:4).
- Ministry of the Word (Acts 6:4).
- Training people for service (Ephesians 4:12).

- Building up the Body of Christ (Ephesians 4:12).
- Guiding the body to unity and maturity (Ephesians 4:13).
- Ruling/governing the people of God (1 Peter 5:2-3).
- Protecting God's people (1 Peter 5:2).
- Caring for and ministering to the people (James 5:14).
- Safeguarding the people from false ministries (1 Timothy 4:1).

Elders activate helps ministries within the congregation by training, approving, assisting, and supervising all persons operating in places of ministry in the Church. Self-appointed "ministers" operate in error, vanity, and rebellion, because they do not submit to supervision and correction. Such persons cause confusion and damage in the house of God. "Parking lot prophets" circulate from church to church and meeting to meeting seeking to give "words from the Lord" both publicly and to individuals. These people, refusing to commit to one local body, can cause tremendous damage while inflating their egos through their "ministries."

It is up to local elders to watch for these people and guard their flock. For this reason, it is wise for all persons operating in gifts and anointings within a local body to submit the practice of those ministers to leadership for approval, correction, and supervision.

Because of the seriousness of eldership responsibilities, it is necessary that elders possess and demonstrate wisdom, stability, and balance. Troubled times demand these qualities from the people who would care for and lead God's people.

Elders in today's church must have a balance of two essential qualities. They must be led by the Holy Spirit and be able to see clearly the vision for ministry God has given them. But, they also must be able to make practical application of the word and vision they have received.

TEAM MINISTRY

Generally, God assigns team leadership to local congregations. Prior to His ascending into heaven, Jesus divided the anointing He possessed and created five separate ministry gifts to continue the work He had begun on earth. No church is complete without at least some exposure to all five of the ministry gifts, because without all five, the full ministry of Jesus as He intended for the Church will not be received.

Team leadership provides for the multitude of counsel. Governing elders can discuss matters of administration and business, and pray together. Gifts of prophecy, administration, and leadership can be blended to implement the will of God in practical ways. Gifts of exhortation, teaching, and prophecy can be utilized to communicate the message to the people. The result is that the work of God can be accomplished effectively.

In Acts 15 the apostles and elders met in Jerusalem to discuss a doctrinal matter; the issue of requiring circumcision and other traditionally Jewish rites among newly converted Gentiles. The Scriptures record that all the apostles and elders were given the opportunity to speak their convictions. Then, when this was done, James, the presiding apostle/elder of the Church, gave his "sentence" in the matter. The principles of counsel among elders was thus established as a primary way to resolve conflict.

Since all five-fold ministers are essentially word ministries, the presence of team ministry can minister a balance of the Word of God from a number of perspectives and approaches. Prophets give words of insight and direction, and evangelists preach the Good News. Teachers explain the Word of God in understandable terms, and pastors feed the flock with messages of encouragement and exhortation. Apostles have a versatile ministry, but usually with respect to an existing church they minister words of correction and application of God's government. All are actively involved in teaching and training the priesthood of all believers for effective service.

Team eldership ensures a greater ability to provide pastoral care for the people. Pastoral and administrative responsibilities can be divided among the team according to preference, gifts, and call. The result of the team approach is that more effective ministry can be accomplished.

The understanding of team ministry must be balanced with the realization that God often imparts the major vision to a single person who is responsible before God to carry out God's will. This person will likely become the primary leader, to be seen as God's person in charge. This does not make the primary leader any better or more important than the others, but it does make him/her the chief among equals. The primary leader will answer to God for the accomplishments of the ministry. His/Her associates must take a supportive role, ministering in terms of the primary leader's vision and goals.

Associates will, however, receive vision and direction from God for their own ministries. When this happens, it must be interpreted in light of the "house" vision and incorporated with the primary leader's overall vision. Many times an associate leader will receive particular insight from the Lord regarding the area of responsibility delegated to him or her. When this happens, the associate's ministry can greatly enhance the mission of the local work.

Leaders must continually seek the delicate balance between operating within their callings and submitting to the vision of the primary leader. Each member of the team will have insight, revelation, and knowledge of the Word. They also will have the strong desire to reach and teach in response to their calling.

The senior leader, however, is the primary voice of the ministry. Otherwise, tension and frustration within a team ministry can occur unless provision is made to allow each member to work out their calling. Mutual understanding is needed to help all team members find fulfillment in their ministries. A team ministry, in order to accomplish the mission of the ministry, must be in unity. There is no place for dissension, strife, confusion, or rebellion. The members must know each other intimately and have a genuine love for each other. Their relationship should not include work time only, but times of fellowship and relaxation as well.

Members of the congregation can readily tell if the leadership team is in unity or not. If the elders are not unified in purpose and function, the people will sense it and become confused or disoriented. Insecurity will develop, and some will leave to find greater security elsewhere.

On the other hand, if the elders function harmoniously through love, the church will become unified, and the people will stand behind their leaders. They will feel secure, and will follow the direction God is leading. Goals will be accomplished and fruitful ministry will eventuate.

The key to the successful operation of a team ministry is communication. Leaders of a ministry must meet often to discuss plans, goals and vision. The senior leader must check in with associates to update them on what they are receiving from God and how to see their goal materialize. They must also listen to what their associates need to tell about their work or what they have heard from God.

Weekly staff meetings are helpful, but not enough. There should be some communication between ministers daily. In a fast-paced world, situations change rapidly. Opportunities for communication between leaders must be established. A communication breakdown can spell disaster for a team ministry – and the Church.

When the elders of a local congregation function in the way God intended them to function, things go well. When the elders follow their own pursuits, become involved in sin, or fail to seek God, their ministry is hindered.

Likewise, when the congregation, for reasons of tradition or lust for power, refuses to allow elders to walk in the anointing and call placed on them, elders find themselves unnecessarily hindered and frustrated in their purposes. Also, they will be unable to freely obey God if all actions are submitted to a governing board for approval.

A delicate balance of trust must be developed to secure the success of the ministry. Members of the local ministry must trust the leadership God has given them, knowing that in the end God will protect them from harm if anything goes wrong. On the other hand, elders must be diligent in seeking God's will for the flock, loving them as dearly as their own families. Love will be demonstrated by the quality of ministry provided.

FUNCTION OF ELDERSHIP

Peter refers to Jesus as the Shepherd and Bishop of our souls, (1 Peter 2:25). He describes Jesus as the Tender of God's flock with functional responsibilities as a Shepherd and a Bishop.

Since New Testament elders are an extension of Jesus' ministry on earth, the same two functions are assigned to church leaders as they minister to God's flock. Elders flow in their respective governmental functions according to calling, gifts, and anointing. Often a team ministry will be evenly divided among these two functions. Both are necessary for the balanced administration of God's work.

Shepherding refers to the act of leading and feeding the people. The aim of one who is called to shepherd is to build up the Body of Christ through healing, edification, comforting, and exhortation. It includes the tasks of pastoral care and evangelism, with specific applications in counseling, preaching, personal ministry, evangelism, missions, and outreach/caring ministries.

The task of shepherding is aimed at bringing the best out of people. Most of the time the function of shepherding is carried out by elders operating as pastors, teachers, or evangelists, often with input from apostles and prophets (preferably).

Utilizing members of the congregation, the leader will call on persons with appropriate spiritual gifts and provide direction and encouragement as they undertake the tasks at hand.

Another word for shepherd with different emphasis is

bishop.[11] Bishops, on the other hand, function in the areas of administration and oversight. In fact, the word, "bishop," is derived from the Greek, *episkopos*, which literally means "overseer." The aim of the bishop is to equip the saints for works of ministry through the tasks of discipleship and government. Specific applications of this ministry include education, training, nurturing, organization, discipline, correction, and administration.

Generally, elders moving in the anointing of apostle, prophet, or teacher will function in the capacity of bishop. A bishop's task is to make sure that administration is carried out in proper form.

DUPLICATION OF LEADERSHIP - ANTIOCH CHURCH

The Bible teaches that elders should train young men to grow into places of leadership. Moses sought God's choice of a successor a number of times before God told him to consecrate Joshua in a special service before the people.

Jesus followed this pattern by choosing twelve men to train and equip during the three and a half years of His ministry. His main focus was to duplicate His ministry in the lives of these twelve men who were later commissioned as apostles to carry on the ministry.

The current trend in the church of sending young men off to seminary has no basis in Scripture. Paul, himself trained in a Jewish institution, the Sanhedrin, did not advocate the practice, but rather, he trained leaders to take his place in the churches he founded. Timothy is an example of this. This is especially seen in the Churches in Antioch and Ephesus.

---

[11] I refer to function, not title.

Local churches can best provide ministerial training for people called into Christian service. Not only are study opportunities available there, but they provide opportunity for first-hand practice in actual ministry.[12]

FELLOWSHIP

Elders should not be limited to their exposure to the local setting. In fact, it is necessary for ministers to have elders beyond the local church setting for supervision, correction, and counsel, as well as fellowship.

MANAGING ELDERS

Pastors can receive valuable leadership assistance from God's people who demonstrate love and devotion for the Lord, as well as spiritual gifts such as administration, leadership, and teaching. Moses himself chose 70 elders from among the congregation to assist him in administration.

One of the best places to use managing elders is in leadership of home fellowship groups. Properly organized, these ministers can give pastoral care to the people in their group, as well as provide valuable feedback from the congregation.

In order to make this work, the senior leader must choose other leaders who will submit to the overall vision of the church. Ideally, they must meet the qualifications for elders set out in 1 Timothy 3 and Titus 1.

The senior leader would meet with managing elders frequently to impart vision and instruction. This can be done through the Council of Elders, which is the assembly of the

---

[12] For more on this important teaching, see the author's book entitled, *Supernatural Architecture*.

pastoral team and the managing elders. It is a time for fellowship, sharing, training, listening, and ministry to the fellowship group leaders.

In the absence of full-time staff, the leader of a small congregation can make use of managing elders to assist him with many areas of ministry. In fact, this position is an excellent training ground for one who senses a call to full time ministry and wants to work toward that goal.

ANTIOCH AND EPHESUS: THE MODEL

> *"...And now brothers, I want to write about the special abilities the Holy Spirit gave to each of you, for I don't want any misunderstanding about them...it is the same and only Holy Spirit who gives all these gifts and powers, deciding which one each of us should have. Our bodies have many parts but the many parts make up only one body when they are put together. So it is with the 'Body of Christ'...each of us is a part of the one Body of Christ..."* (1 Corinthians 12:1-13, Living N.T.).

This passage of Scripture is the clearest single group of Scriptures concerning the need for administration in the local church expression. Paul tells the Corinthian church that everyone in the Body of Christ has gifts and a place of function, but the Holy Spirit also has explicit instruction from the Father that without some form of structure or guidance, members of the Body would have difficulty identifying their manifestation of the gifts and their proper function or finding their place. This is clearly illustrated in verses 15-17 of the same chapter.

THE CHURCH MUST HAVE QUALIFIED ELDERS/LEADERS

The first requirement of a family is parents. To gather

a flock and feed them requires a shepherd (or shepherds). To produce a "household of faith" requires the oversight of spiritual parents. These women/men should be called as one of the five-fold ministries of Ephesians 4:11-12 and meet the requirements of elders.

If these requirements are not met, or if they are compromised, it will be seen in the fruit of the work. To try and build a church on those who do not spiritually qualify will always produce a frustration for shepherd and sheep alike.

The leader (or leaders) should be well established in God's word with demonstrated maturity. He/She must then impart from the word. He must be able to feed and edify the flock so they are spiritually content. Feeding is the heart of the ministry. Good government can never exist where there is an inability of the leaders to feed properly. *"Where there is no vision the people perish."*

It must be understood that the Spirit leads and governs the Church through human beings. To bypass everyone and seek to be led by "God only" is a fallacy, is usually a sign of a rebellious and independent person. This rebellious, independent spirit is a part of our national heritage in America, and is most often seen in independent churches (churches that do not belong to any denomination or fellowship of churches). Even in the Old Testament, God led His people through men. God leads and governs His church by His Spirit through men and women, called and gifted for servant leadership (Hebrews 13:17; Ephesians 4:11, etc.). Notice the importance of the supervisory ministry and frequency of its mention in the New Testament.

The balanced pattern of the Scripture. There are some fine lines which must be distinguished in grappling with various concepts of God's direct government. This has been an issue from ancient times. The thing to avoid in attempting to find a specific biblical pattern is missing God and replacing Him with something non-biblical.

Both the democratic form of government (consensus of opinion) and dictatorship (one man/one woman rule) can be equally humanistic instead of godly.

Let us consider, from the Word of God, examples of how God brought balance through His leader who worked in a yoke of plurality with fellow leaders.

The One (singular) Leader Working With The Plurality

Moses and the elders	Exodus 3:16-18
Joshua and the elders	Joshua 7:6
Samuel and the elders	1 Samuel 8:3-4
Saul and the elders	1 Samuel 15:30
David and the elders	2 Samuel 5:3
Solomon and the elders	2 Kings 8:1-3
Josiah and the elders	2 Chronicles 34:29
Ezra and the elders	Ezra 10:8-14
Ezekiel and the elders	Ezekiel 8:1
Peter and the elders	1 Peter 5:1-4
Peter and the apostles	Acts 15:2, 14
James and the apostles	Acts 15
Paul and the elders	Acts 19:20
Timothy and the elders	1 Timothy 3
Titus and the elders	Titus 1:5

From this we see that God's pattern is to put His mantle of Fatherhood leadership upon certain ones who, by virtue of their calling, rise up and make room for other ministries and offices.

THE APOSTLE AND THE ELDER

There are two key ministries in the reproductive cycle of the church: the apostle and the elder (Acts 13:1-4).

> *"Now there were in the church that was at Antioch, certain prophets and teachers..."* (five men are named who held the ministry function of prophets and teachers, among whom are Barnabas and Saul or Paul, v. 1)

> *"As they ministered to the Lord and fasted, the Holy Ghost said* (prophetic utterance) *separate unto me Barnabas and Saul for the work whereunto I have called them"* (v. 2).

Before Barnabas and Paul were sent forth from the believers at Antioch, they were among the **prophets** and **teachers**.

After they were sent forth they were known as "**sent-forth ones**" or "**apostles**" (Acts 14:4, 14). In the course of their journey they visited the city of Lystra. On their second visit they "ordained"[13] elders in the Church in Antioch (Acts 14:21-23).

Level 1:	Barnabas	-	Antioch
Level 2:	Paul	-	Antioch
Level 3:	Silas	-	Ephesus
Level 4:	Timothy	-	Lystra
Level 5:	Titus	-	Crete

---

[13] Greek:*cheirotoneo* - literally the approbation and recognition by putting forth the hand as a result of manifesting themselves as gifted of God to discharge the functions of elders.

Here we see the apostolic ministry being brought forth out of fellowship, and being received by those of kindred fellowship.

The second stage takes place in Lystra. Within the local congregation, **apostles ordain the elders** who thereafter assume responsibility for the leadership of that congregation.

After completing their journey, Paul and Barnabas returned to Antioch and reported to the congregation which originally sent them forth (Acts 14:26-28). In due course, Paul was sent forth a second time, taking with him Silas, a prophet (Acts 15:32, 40).

Acts 16:1 describes how Paul, accompanied by Silas, goes to Lystra and finds a young man named Timothy, who has a good commendation (v. 2). Paul desired Timothy to join them (v. 3-4). Here we see both Silas and Timothy, from local congregations, given good commendations and being made "sent-forth ones" or apostles. 1 Thessalonians 1:1 and 2:6 describe these three apostles.

Timothy received his recognition publicly at the presbytery gathering (1 Timothy 4:14; 2 Timothy 1:6). The presbytery was the gathering of the elders, including Paul and Silas, and recognized ministries.

In a later phase of their travels, Paul and Timothy came to the city of Ephesus. They ministered together for some period of time. Then Paul moved on leaving Timothy to finish some work which still needed to be done. (Acts 19:1-22; 1 Timothy 1:3).

From 1 Timothy 3:1-10 and 5:17-22 we learn that Timothy's main task was to appoint elders. From Titus 1:5-9 we see that on another occasion, Titus was left by Paul in

Crete with a similar responsibility, that of appointing elders. Timothy, as an **apostle**, has come to Ephesus and has **appointed elders** in the congregation in that city. Now the way is open for the elders of Ephesus to send forth the next apostolic company (not described in scripture). This depicts the reproductive cycle which should continue until the Lord returns.

There are governmental offices and spiritual ministries in the Church. Scripture recognizes only two governmental offices in each local church. These are elders and deacons. Let us look briefly at the functions of each.

ELDER'S FUNCTIONS

He must help **shepherd the flock of God** (1 Peter 5:2; Acts 20:28; 1 Timothy 3:5). That is, he must care for the church. Like a shepherd who oversees a flock of sheep, he is to guard the people of God against false teachers (Acts 20:28-30). He is to meet their needs and assist them in whatever way he can.

He is not to **lord it over those allotted to his charge, but he is to be an example to the flock** (1 Peter 5:3). He is not to use his position for selfish gain or to exhibit dictatorial attitudes. Rather, he is to lead by example, obviously a Christ-like example.

He is to **teach** and **exhort** (1 Timothy 3:2; Titus 1:9).

He is to stand up and expose those who teach false doctrine and to teach sound doctrine (Titus 1:11). Part of the shepherding responsibility is to **feed the flock** of God.

He is to **manage the church of God** (1 Timothy 3:5), that is, to oversee the Church Body and administer the affairs of the Church. They are to be men who "rule well" (Greek *proistemi* – literally, to be over, superintend, go before). There is a comparison made here in 1 Timothy 5:17-18 between those elders who do not exhibit equal capacity or efficiency in ruling. (The text in the Greek does not support the Reformed Theory of two classes of elders – ruling and teaching.) Those who rule well are to be given double honor (literally, more than adequate remuneration) hence the warning not to take this task for the sake of "filthy lucre" (1 Peter 5:2).

He is to **pray for the sick** (James 5:14-15). That is, along with the other elders of the church, he is to go where the sick are and pray for their spiritual and physical well-being.

DEACON'S FUNCTIONS

A second leader that is mentioned in the New Testament in relationship to the local church is a **deacon**. The word in Greek, *diakonos*, literally means "servant," and it is from this meaning of the word that we must determine the **function** of those who have this leadership position.

Deacons are referred to only in Paul's letter to the Philippians (1:1) and his first letter to Timothy (3:8-12). In one case the character is implied and in the other the function. The closest we can come to a specific reference is Acts 6 where 7 men were appointed to serve tables (The word deacon is not used in Acts 6, but the word "to serve" actually comes from the same root word as the word translated "deacon"). This passage, although used by many to justify giving deacons menial and material tasks only, illustrates a temporary task that needed attention in the church. When the Church was scattered, so were the seven. The communal system was no longer continued and there is no further reference to this function in Scripture. One must come to the conclusion in studying the churches of the New

Testament that not all had elders and deacons. Some, it appears, had only elders while others had both. The needs of the flock must determine the multiplication of leadership, both elders and deacons.

Paul implies in 1 Timothy 3:10 that the deacons as well as the elders must first be proved. The Greek word for "be proved," *dokimazo*, literally means, "to put to the test for the purpose of approving, and having met the test to be approved." The test does not refer to a formal examination, but has reference to the general judgment of the Christian community as to whether or not they fulfill the qualifications set down in the Word. (Bear in mind, both Stephen and Philip exercised a far greater ministry than modern deacons.)

Together the elders and deacons should provide the day-to-day leadership of the local church. Above the elders there is no higher level of administrative leadership. If we are to preserve the autonomy and integrity of the local church, we must never depart from **two basic principles**: first, there is no governmental office above the eldership, and second, the eldership that emerges must be plural. A work that continues too long under one man will never function in God's ultimate purposes. **Plurality must emerge as the flock increases.**

The spiritual ministries sent out from the local church – apostles, prophets, evangelists and teachers were always subject to the elders wherever they went, and of course had no right to exercise governmental authority over another assembly. In 3 John 9-10, Diotrephes refused the brethren entrance to the assembly and John the beloved Apostle had to grant respect to his actions, although he gave stern warning against him.

These ministries were also obligated to return to their assemblies and give account of their activities, e.g., Paul and Barnabas returned to Antioch to give account in Acts 14:26-28.

In conclusion, let us reaffirm that God does not ordain or sanction the lawlessness of those who exalt themselves into ministry functions and titles.

Many men today in the current outpouring of the Holy Spirit have been given gifts by God for the edification of the Church and the evangelization of the lost. The tragedy of our hour is that so many are seeking to function outside God's order and they will face the Lord Jesus in judgment as revealed in Matthew 7:21-23. They will profess they have done much, but Jesus has declared that, unless we flow in His divine order, we are workers of iniquity and lawlessness.

God wants to bring forth His glory, but only through those who will submit to His Word. Again we reaffirm that God's pattern as consistently revealed in the Scriptures, is to place a mantle of leadership or fatherhood upon one who is available and called by God. Then as the work progresses under the hand of the shepherd, other "under-shepherds" are raised up to share the burden and responsibility of the flock.

"Leadership is action, not position."
Davey Crockett

"The ultimate measure of a man is not where he stands in moments of comfort and convenience, but where he stands at times of challenge and controversy"
Martin Luther King, Jr.

"You can't lead anyone else further than you have gone yourself." Gene Mauch

CHAPTER 8

A CALL TO COMMITMENT

"Now, therefore, fear the LORD and serve Him in sincerity and truth; and put away the gods which your fathers served beyond the River and in Egypt, and serve the LORD. If it is disagreeable in your sight to serve the LORD, choose for yourselves today whom you will serve: whether the gods which your fathers served which were beyond the River, or the gods of the Amorites in whose land you are living; but as for me and my house, we will serve the LORD." The people said to Joshua, "No, but we will serve the LORD" (Joshua 24:14-15, 21).

We are in a war against evil satanic forces. To fight a war requires commitment, competence, and courage. In the Scripture reference above, though this was one of the most faithful generations, it had to be called to further commitment.

What God desires is voluntary commitment. Our best examples are Joshua's challenge to the people (Joshua 24:14-21).

We also see that Moses chose suffering with the people of God:

"By faith Moses, when he was come to years, refused to be called the son of Pharoah's daughter; choosing rather to suffer affliction with the people of God, than to enjoy the pleasures of sin for a

season; esteeming the reproach of Christ greater riches than the treasures in Egypt...for he endured, as seeing him who is invisible. Through faith he kept the passover, and the sprinkling of blood, lest he that destroyed the first-born should touch them" (Hebrews 11:24-28).

God only commands those who are willing. Only those who want to, will obey Him.

Commitment Requires Contentment

God further desires you to be content where you are. *"Not that I speak from want, for I have learned to be content in whatever circumstances I am"* (Philippians 4:11).

You belong where you are if there is no other clear direction. If you are not content where you are, you'll never be content where you go. You belong where you are if there is no indication that it should be otherwise. 1 Corinthians 16:9, *"...for a wide door for effective service has opened to me."*

David served his men and his men served him. Absalom conned the people and they soon returned to his father (Acts 13:36). For David, after he had served his own generation by the will of God, he slept with his fathers in peace.

Commitment Deplores Contention

The Church is not an abstract thing. We are related to people. Sheep respond to tender loving care. Relationship in the house must be founded on love. Thus, leaders must stand with people during hard times, as well as good! (Jeremiah 33:12-13).

God desires that you be committed to a team. God's house was never built on loners. You must be joined to others in the Body to function correctly with maximum benefit (Ephesians 4:16).

> *"But Paul kept insisting that they should not take him along who had deserted them in Pamphylia and had not gone with them to the work"* (Acts 15:38).

To contrast this, fools do that which is right in their own eyes, while kings confer (Proverbs 12:15). Also, a wise leader will not use a loner (one who will not accept counsel, Proverbs 12:10). Pride brings contention/division (Proverbs 1:20-33).

In Proverbs we read:

> *"Trust in the LORD with all your heart and do not lean on your own understanding. In all your ways acknowledge Him, and He will make your paths straight"* (Proverbs 3:5-6).

There are so many things in which we can attempt to place our confidence. Our hope and security must be in God's good hands. There are crutches that leaders may use which will not stand the test of time. All are poor substitutes for God's grace being applied through a committed life. These include:

Our abilities (Jeremiah 10:23). We are to be well trained and capable, yet we dare not trust in our professionalism, eloquence or giftedness. All of these can fail us.

Our knowledge or education (John 3:27; Proverbs 10:14; 24:5; Romans 10:2; 1 Corinthians 8:1; Ephesians 3:19). Educational achievement is a worthy pursuit, as long as it is kept in proper perspective. In the passages referenced we see the importance of knowledge (wise men store it up and it increases power). The Scripture warns, however, that the misappropriation of knowledge can create arrogance and is inferior to love. Our confidence should not be in our education or degrees but in the Lord.

Our achievements (2 Corinthians 3:5). Paul understood that all he had was a gift from the Lord. Standing on our own laurels can prove to be very shaky ground.

Our place in society (Matthew 23:1-12). The Pharisees were hated for taking the place of prominence in the sight of men. Jesus condemned them for their hypocrisy. Jesus calls us to a committed servanthood, not the lap of luxury. Prosperity is a gift from the Lord (as are all good gifts) and should be enjoyed, appreciated and shared.

Our friends, self, or riches (Proverbs 11:28; 2 Corinthians 1:9; Proverbs 29:25). Putting our confidence in anything other than the Lord will not last. Money in the bank can be devalued, our talents may wane, our friends may be as bad as Job's, but the Lord will never forsake us.

We must learn as men and women of God to trust in the Lord and His grace for the fulfillment of our call. It is only through fully trusting in the Lord and in the parts of the body who have proven themselves trustworthy, that we can be truly effective for the Lord.

A TIME TO DELEGATE

As a leader you have two choices in doing your work. When a task has been assigned to you, you can either do it yourself or get someone to do it. Your ability to enlist others to share in the task, to delegate effectively, is going to determine your success. Your position and rate of promotion, your pay, your status, prestige, and success in management, or your role as spiritual leader will be determined by your ability to delegate properly.

Mr. Andrew Carnegie was one of the best at the art of delegation. At one time he had thirty-four millionaires working for him. They were a lot smarter than he, yet he had made them millionaires. He could spot potential and develop it into leadership material. He said, "I owe whatever success I have attained by and large to my ability to surround myself with people who are smarter than I am (Andrew Carnegie)."

Leaders have two major weaknesses which, if they conquer, will free them to become excellent leaders. They are:

- The inability to develop people under them and release them.
- The willingness to share the ministry with capable, imperfect people.

CREDIBILITY

We will look at both of these in turn. We must learn the power of delegation and begin to train people under us. When we study successful people, the spiritual and secular world shows us this: The men who make the most money, or have successful organizations, very seldom do the work themselves.

How many hours can you work and how much money can you make? The men who make the most money don't necessarily work more hours. They have learned to select and motivate key associates to help carry the load and complete the majority of the tasks.

Our ability to delegate comes through a growth process.

As we grow older we learn we can't do it all ourselves

and be effective. After enough trial and error or experience in finding out what works and what doesn't we become much more secure in passing to others work that is essential, but where our energies are not maximal.

All great leaders have learned the art of delegation; in fact, excellent leadership is synonymous with it. If a person does not learn this art, two things will likely happen, both of them negative.

That person will limit the amount of responsibility that he or she can handle, thus limiting their future growth.

He will inhibit the initiative of those under him, limiting the efficiency of the entire group.

People who do not have the ability to delegate have significant difficulty and increased stress.

If a person doesn't have the ability to develop and delegate under their leadership, the quality people will soon grow frustrated and leave because quality people always look for new worlds to conquer. If they can't develop under our leadership, they will go somewhere else where they can.

There are nine main reasons why people do not delegate. They are:

- Insecurity, or a lack of confidence in one's gift and call.
- Lack of ability to train others, often due to one's own poor or inadequate training.
- The lack of confidence in others, or an inability to trust them.
- There is no one qualified to assist. This is often true in smaller or new churches. In fact, wisdom dictates

patience in choosing leaders until faithfulness is shown.

- Personal enjoyment of a task, where you do not want to "give way."
- Past failures or bad experiences that are unresolved.
- Not enough time, making it easier to do it yourself (bad planners).
- Expectation of others.
- Pastors (leaders) do so much because people expect it of them.

Then we must educate church people in understanding the role and function of the ministry.

There are some myths that keep people from delegating. Poor delegators believe that there is not enough time to delegate. Secondly, they believe the person is not competent enough for the job. Third is the myth that if you want it done right, you must do it yourself. Fourth, people might think that I'm not on top of the job if I have to delegate. Finally, if you're good at it, you should do it. But the truth is whatever you have mastered; delegate it, so you can move on to higher levels of responsibility and authority.

THE PROCESS

So how does one delegate? The process of delegation will be determined by your ability to do four things:

1) Choose, 2) Communicate, 3) Control, 4) Coach

CHOOSE

It has been said that timing is everything. The time to delegate is when you are missing deadlines, or doing something someone else can do. Also, if crises are frequent in your own life, it causes an imbalance of time and priorities. It may be time to delegate.

Communicate

We must communicate the value or worth to the individual you have chosen for delegation.

Their value or worth to the ministry, their family and those that they will lead is essential. Nothing motivates a person you have chosen as leader more than this. This elevates them. You must be able to communicate the need of a project and the importance of the person, and the value or importance of the project for the person.

Control

Control is another important aspect of delegation. Successful delegation involves territory or recognizing the needs we all have to claim our own space, knowing that when we give a person a territory or space, they will do better with it. When you delegate, you do not just give responsibility but the authority to act as your representative. As we are to be ambassadors for Christ, so the one to whom we delegate must have the authority to act in our absence.

There Is A Basic Premise To Control

It is fruitless to attempt to control the way people do their jobs. It is not possible anyway. Everyone does a job in their own style. The function of a supervisor is to analyze results rather than try to control how the task is completed. The goal to do the job – how it is done (as long as it is legal and ethical) is up to the worker; give them freedom to demonstrate competence.

THERE ARE TWO TYPES OF CONTROL

First, tight control which is needed when either the project, or the person assigned, is still an unknown. If you want to maintain control while giving power to others, don't give them full reign immediately. Ease them into authority, correcting their behavior as they go along. You would thus delegate in steps as suggested here.

Ask them to be fact-finders only, rather than taking on the full project, so you can see how well they handle a less critical portion. Ask them to make suggestions that can help. Further, ask them to implement one of their recommendations, but only after you have given approval to them. Ask them to take action on their own, but to report the results immediately. Ultimately, when faithfulness is demonstrated, give them complete authority. This is the way to delegate, step by step.

The advantages of tight control are that it can make up for any deficiency in people and provides opportunity to train them. This is effective when initiative and creativity are needed.

Light control can be used when a person has proven ability. One of the advantages of light control is that it frees the leader to handle more important responsibilities and allows creativity for the person to whom the job is delegated.

In delegating, the three essential elements must be given: Responsibility to be given by you to accomplish the task, authority to act as an ambassador, and accountability to the leadership.

The benefits of delegation result in an increase in output and the ability to concentrate on things that are of value in the ministry. Through it you will see growth in those under shepherds or the young Timothys that will hopefully mature into future leaders for the Body of Christ.

COACH - MOBILIZING THE PEOPLE

The Bible says that the job of leaders is to "equip the saints for the work of the ministry" (Ephesians 4:12). This is so that persons can fulfill their Christian witness and at the same time help the senior leaders focus on their calling. This is done through a ministry termed by the New Testament as *diakonia*, which means "service, a commission or ministry in the service of the gospel, the act of rendering friendly offices" (Moulton, H. ed. 1977). This ministry began in Acts 6 when the apostles became frustrated with the amount of work they were doing to keep things going. Peter called the church's attention to the fact that they were neglecting the Word and prayer in order to wait on tables, and had the people nominate persons to take the responsibility of feeding widows (Acts 6:1-7). Peter told them that after the matter was settled he and the other apostles would be able to *"give ourselves continually to prayer, and to the ministry of the word."*

The deaconate emerged from Christ's own ministry just as did the ministry of the elder. Paul writes that he made himself a servant (*diakonos*) and slave. Further, he declared to the disciples that whoever would be the greatest among them must first be the servant, or deacon of all (Stam, D. 1975). The deacon ministry became a specific office within the church, when certain members answered the call for positions of service. Authority was extended to them so that they could accomplish the work at hand (Acts 6:3).

SUMMARY AND CONCLUSIONS

Today there are many types of church government

within the Body of Christ. While each may have some small portion of what was originally intended for the Church, it is safe to say that by and large church government intended by God (if it can be known from New Testament writings) has been all but forgotten. Traditional approaches have taken the place of God's perfect plan.

God has given us patterns to use in the Scriptures. Just as one purchases a sewing pattern which may produce five or six completely different outfits, God has given the Church a pattern which can be adjusted and fitted to meet the needs of given local situations.

The pattern includes an emphasis on order, vision, the Word of God, and the Kingdom of God, worship, prayer, and fellowship (Acts 2:42). It calls for plural leadership from seasoned men appointed by God who sit in council together. It includes an understanding of community, commitment, and discipleship. And most important, it includes an awareness that Jesus Christ is Lord and that this is His Church called for His purposes to accomplish His plans. But, one thing is certain. It is time for all leaders to understand God's patterns (not specific laws), and with wisdom adjust to His plan.

"Pray as if everything depended upon God and work as if everything depended upon man." Francis Joseph Spellman

"The true measure of a man is not the number of servants he has, but the number of people he serves." Arnold Glasgow

"The best executive is the one who has sense enough to pick good men to do what he wants done, and self-restraint to keep from meddling with them while they do it." Theodore Roosevelt

CHAPTER 9

CHURCH GOVERNMENT AND ADMINISTRATION

DEFINITION OF GOVERNMENT

Government refers to the system which keeps the elements of life in order. Government is the means of providing stability and security in all creation.

The universe functions by a set of natural laws. These laws keep the planets from colliding in space, provide for weather, and give the world its physical characteristics and properties. The moment God spoke creation into existence, these physical laws were enacted and government of the physical elements began.

Government is applied to and by man in a number of ways. It can be defined as the exercise of authority, control, rule, or management over a person or group of persons. It also can be defined as a system of ruling, controlling, or exercising authority, as well as a system of political administration.

God is the Author and Creator of all government, and it exists for the benefit of man. Paul writes in Romans 13 that God has established all human authorities to provide political and social stability. Paul says these authorities have been given for the benefit of man, to provide a sense of normality and stability in the interactions amongst individuals and communities.

Government is in reality a blessing of God. It not only includes rules and limitations, but it also involves instruction, blessing, and freedom to operate within a framework of security.

God has established government in His Church to keep things in order. He desires for His people to walk in the freedom and excitement of the callings and giftings He has placed within each one. Local church government is provided by God to provide the best conditions possible for each individual to carry on kingdom ministry.

THE KINGDOM OF GOD[14]

In Scripture, the style of government God has established for the Church is described by the word, kingdom. Simply stated, the Kingdom of God refers to man's submission to God as the undisputed authority of the Church and the practical application of His will. The kingdom operates through the delegates he has called, ordained, and anointed.

The First Century Church developed a kingdom government through the leadership of apostles and prophets. However, since the apostolic founders passed from the scene man has developed ecclesiastical systems of government according to his own understanding or according to the patterns of prevailing political governments of the world.

Careful study of the scriptures reveals that God has established the theocratic pattern of government for His people. In every case where man allowed God to govern as He saw fit there was peace, prosperity, and stability among the people of God.

The government of the kingdom is different from all the

---

[14] See more in *That's the Kingdom.*

other forms mentioned here in that it cannot be operated by man in the flesh. It cannot be operated by carnal believers who never seek the mind of God, no matter how gifted or well-intentioned they are.

Kingdom government operates as men seek the will and way of God for the direction of the Church. It calls for men to put aside their own preferences and ideas to submit to the Lordship of Jesus Christ as the head of all things.

Personal holiness and a heart for God are the prerequisites for those who would seek a place in God's system of government. It is said David was chosen king of God's people because he was a man after God's own heart.

PLURAL MINISTRY IN THE NEW TESTAMENT

Jesus' appointment of five ministry gifts indicates a division of ministry tasks into five areas, thus creating the need for a plural ministry. Jesus, in effect, divided His own ministry role among several men who must work together in unison to obtain the full expression of the ministry of Jesus.

GIFTS TO THE BODY

As previously stated, the helps ministry was established early in the development of the New Testament Church. Acts 6:1-7 records Peter's frustration with the situation, and his decision to appoint Godly, spirit-filled men to work in these places of service.

The Deacon ministry, as developed in the early church, is a helping ministry to elders as they serve the people. There is no scriptural precedent for deacon boards which have an active role in directing the church's ministry and administration.

SUCCESSION OF LEADERSHIP IN THE NEW TESTAMENT

It is clear that personal discipleship was the method of training future leaders in the New Testament. Jesus chose and taught the twelve over a period of three and a half years before sending them out in their ministries. Paul trained Timothy and Titus as apostolic leaders and left them in charge of their respective churches.

SUMMARY

Basically, the pattern we see in both Testaments is that God ordains a primary leader, giving him the vision, call, anointing, and responsibility for the task of governing God's people. The primary leader is given associate leaders, or governing elders, to share the load of the governmental function, but always within the anointing and vision of the primary leader.

In God's plan, the Gentiles were grafted in as a part of God's chosen people. Our pattern should remain as developed by our Hebrew tradition, not Greek dualistic or Ecclesiastical patterns. This pattern is best seen in the ministry of the Apostle Paul in the establishment of the church in Antioch.[15]

GOVERNMENT IN THE CHURCH

All authority comes from God (Romans 13:1). Authority (*exousia* in Greek) flows from the heart of God, can be seen in all nature, was given to Christ, and transferred to and through His apostles unto our present day. Authority and government is absolutely necessary in the local church.

The function of government is essential in that biblical government will restrain injustice and lawlessness,

---

[15] For more on this concept, see *Supernatural Architecture* by Dr. DeKoven.

bring discipline to the unruly, and create unity for the people of God. In fact, the key to church government is unity, or dwelling together with one purpose (Psalm 133:1). God's anointing flows from top to bottom under authority and wherever order has been established. However, this is not to say that everything must be controlled legislatively, but under the order found in God's Word and as led by the Holy Spirit (which will never contradict the written Word).

The unity of government must be voluntary, not demanded by leaders. Where voluntary submission to the local church occurs authority is established. This leads to a release of the power (dunamis) of God for service; evangelism, and so on (See Acts 2:42).

MINISTRIES AND GIFTS

Under the authority of the local church the gifts of the Spirit (1 Corinthians 12:11-12; Romans 12:3-8) are to function in harmony. It is God Himself who has appointed these gifts in the Church (1 Corinthians 12:28), and it is God's plan that under five-fold ministry authority they function properly in the Church.

PRINCIPLES OF ORGANIZATION 1

The local church is designed to be self-governing, self-supporting and under proper scriptural authority which is instituted by God. The scriptural authority is found in the Church in Antioch and the ministry of Paul (Acts 13) and in his letters to his disciples. We further see this in Paul's letter to his sons in the faith.

God's Word speaks of an organized local church guided by qualified leadership. Those qualifications have already been described and are summarized in Appendix 1. Paul admonished his disciples to set the house of God in order to ensure that unity was established, acknowledging their direct responsibility to God while being open to what the Spirit was saying to the Church through each member. There was a plurality of elders with a chief amongst equals who moved the congregation according to the direction of the Lord.

These newly established churches were effective because they were formed and established by the Holy Spirit. Each local body was autonomous, yet in mutual submission to one another due to relationship. The leadership encouraged the ministry gifts to function in the local body, and every believer was trained and released into service according to the apostolic pattern that they had learned.

Ultimately, a church established with a strong foundation remained strong through the raising up of elders, deacons and ministries which had to learn to flow together in balance according to the ultimate law of love and mutual relational submission.

PRINCIPLES OF ORGANIZATION 2

Gene Edwards in his somewhat controversial book on church history, points out the dynamics of the first century church. On the Day of Pentecost the church grew from 120 to 3,120!

At that time there were none of the modern "necessities" for church planting and growth that we rely on today. They had no meeting place for these 3,000 new converts (all of whom were seekers of God, it is assumed most did not live or work in Jerusalem!).

They used Solomon's porch (behind the temple) for teaching. They had no Bibles, no public address system, no bulletins, no music ministry. However, they did have the apostles who had imprinted in their hearts, minds and spirits the pattern of discipleship demonstrated by Jesus Himself.

Thus, the need for organization began the day after the birth of the Church. Lodging had to be found, meeting places determined (house to house), teaching began, and the work of ministry, initially done only by the apostles, was inaugurated.

In the midst of this outpouring of God's Spirit, the Church began the process of organizing itself to function in unity.

THE CHURCH GROWS

As the church grew, the work of ministry became more intense. The apostles not only ministered the Word but also (apparently) cared for physical needs. Eventually there was a need for deacons, elders, and the other ministries as discussed in Romans, Corinthians and Ephesians.

The work of organizing a church is to be done as the need arises, and in the timing of the Lord. To select leaders for the sake of it can lead to disorder. In all things the organization should follow biblical patterns and follow the leading of the Holy Spirit. It starts with the vision, and continues with planning and goal setting.

PLANNING AND GOAL ESTABLISHMENT

During a rather difficult leadership meeting a pastor was asked about his plan for the fulfillment of the "vision" for the local church. His "vision" was to "win the city" for Jesus (certainly an excellent, though somewhat grandiose, desire) through this one local church. The pastor's response was, "I'll preach and God will make it happen."

Unfortunately, this naive pastor had no idea about the task of leadership, nor the biblical mandate of planning and organization. For no matter how great a preacher might be, a leader must do more than just preach, he must plan and set goals that puts meat on the bones of the vision.

THE PLAN

Long before a church is planted a plan must be established. Though the Lord can and has spontaneously begun churches (see Antioch), most are done according to a plan that flows from a vision.

In establishing a plan, one must first define what the church will be like when it is established. The planner must have a certain amount of end results in mind with a focus on the who, what, when, where, how and why of the future church or ministry. The question that is asked is where does God want this work in one, three, five or ten years?

All details must be included in the plan (which must be in writing) to include who will lead the project, when to begin, what will be the cost, facilities needed, possible hindrances, etc.

Obviously Paul the Apostle did not leave on his missionary journeys with his knapsack and a Bible. He planned his journeys, and his plans were submitted to the wisdom of the elders (whom he reported back to, Acts 14) and to the leading of the Holy Spirit. Goal planning will follow steps similar to those presented here.

DEFINING THE PROJECT

The project, whether an outreach, a new ministry, a short-term missions project or a church plant, must be clearly defined. This is presented in the form of a statement that includes the specific goal.

DEVELOP THE PROCESS

The process of developing the project includes the definition and continues by bringing together people of like heart to discuss and develop the plan. I am not a strong advocate of committees, but having three to five people who can bounce sanctified ideas off each other in brainstorming sessions can be very dynamic. The actual plan comes through these brainstorming sessions, as will the procedures to be followed. It is helpful to have a spokesperson that will present the proposed plan to the leadership of the church or ministry as it is developed.

SPECIFIC DETAILS

The plan must include the personnel needed to make the project successful. For instance, a church needs more than just a pastor. It requires helps-ministry, music, evangelism, and education (especially a children's ministry). Thus, a team is usually better than an individual or couple in starting a major project. Though Paul may have been able to inaugurate single-handedly a church, he always had supporters who came with him, who provided needed assistance in the development of ministry.

Further, the cost of the project must be determined. Jesus stated that no man sets out to erect a building without first counting the cost (Luke 14:18-30). Most projects which fail do so because of poor selection of personnel and a lack of finances. Chuck Smith, the founder of the Calvary Chapels, has been quoted to say that what God gives in terms of vision, God will give in provision. Certainly there is always a certain amount of faith involved in every project and God can and often does make miraculous provision. However, this must be balanced by proper planning, including the financial commitment to ensure that a project will be completed.

The Time Factor

Everything takes time. Most leaders are in a hurry, but God never is. In our planning, a projected time frame should be established. If past experience is any indication of future projections, everything takes more time than we think. Thus, we need to be realistic, yet hopeful, in our planning, always submitting our plans to the Lord.

The Promotion

Finally, once a plan and goals (which are measurable and obtainable) are established, it must be whole-heartedly promoted by the leadership. If the promotion does not occur from the present leadership, it will have great difficulty in becoming established.

The promotion should be in writing, exclaimed verbally and enthusiastically. Commitments should be obtained by the people to support the vision and the plan, and the project needs to remain in front of the people until the project is a reality.

Basic Church Administration

Whether we like it or not, a majority of our time in ministry is spent in the administration of the Church. In the city, administration is usually the weakest area of ministry.

The focus of most city churches is in preaching and teaching, yet the ultimate growth of the Church is determined upon principles of stewardship or administration.

THE WORD AND ADMINISTRATION

In 1 Corinthians 12:27-28 the word "governments" or "administration" is spoken of (Greek word, *kubernesis*) as an appointed ministry or gift. What a blessing a pastor has if he/she has a trained and anointed administrator in the Church. An administrator is a manager who works to bring about the successful completion of a task. They give guidance to and regulate the task until accomplished, and in doing so help to facilitate the vision of the Lord for a local church.

Without proper administration, the Church can become chaotic. Ultimately, it is the apostle that sets the Church in order. Yet, the apostle is rarely able to administer the day-to-day operations. He/she is not called or gifted for long-term administration. Neither is the pastor who has the focus on people rather than projects.

There is a need for a trained and effective administrator for growth. However, the spiritual leader must know and understand principles of administration to know if things are being done *"decently and in order"* (1 Corinthians 14:20). Ignorance is not bliss!

THE IMPORTANCE OF DELEGATION

Though stated in depth previously, the leadership in the local church, the five-fold ministry, needs to be willing to delegate their authority and responsibility to faithful men and women who are biblically qualified to serve. Earlier in this book the important characteristics of a delegated leader are listed. An administrator is a delegated leader with a focus on organizing and ensuring the implementation of the vision, purpose, goals and plans of the leadership, and actively participates in the planning of the local church.

Many areas of service are touched by a good administrator.

Assist in Goal-Setting, Planning, and Meetings

An administrator helps to keep things on task. He/she will assist in setting intermediate and short-term goals as part of achieving longer-term goals. Further, they will plan and establish agendas for meetings designed to discuss and decide direction. Once direction is decided, the administrator will help to establish the systems necessary to ensure implementation of the goals or decisions made. They are "how-to" people, who often delegate to others specific tasks of an individual nature, while tracking progress and ensuring completion of tasks in a prescribed time frame.

Organizing

The administrator will, in coordination with the senior leader, develop policies and procedures for the smooth flow of the office and activities of the ministry. The policies will cover staff relations, office hours, telephone procedures, job descriptions, sick/vacation policies and procedures, dress code, etc. Usually the administrator will develop a policy and procedure manual which covers the above and hiring/firing policies, performance appraisals, pay and benefits, etc. Finally, a good administrator will pull together the various ends of the ministry and ensure that the parts are functioning in unity. Obviously, this is no easy task. That's why most leaders of ministries are in prayer for an associate/administrator who can take this burden. Without good administration from proper incorporation to tax planning, from project plans to general paperwork, the ministry of Christ can be in jeopardy.

"Leadership is getting someone to do what they don't want to do, to achieve what they want to achieve." Tom Landry

"Surround yourself with the best people you can find, delegate authority, and don't interfere." Ronald Reagan

"Nearly all men can stand adversity, but if you want to test a man's character, give him power." Abraham Lincoln

CHAPTER 10

THE LEADER IN RELATIONSHIP

Relationship is important to God. As vividly seen in the Trinity, God is intimate in relationship from the start. As with God, leaders need each other, perhaps not more than ever.

Jesus chose twelve. He had an inner circle of intimates, including John, the one he loved (at least according to John). Paul began with rigid rules for his co-laborers, but near the end of his life cared more about quality friends than the failures of the past (e.g., John Mark).

All leaders need healthy relationships, both peers and followers. We cannot accomplish the work of God alone.

In the early church, the Holy Spirit chose men and women for leadership. As the church expanded beyond Jerusalem the Lord moved upon Paul the Apostle to place them in positions of relational authority, for the blessing and protection of the people of God. When Paul placed them in (elders and deacons) in office, he admonished them concerning their duties. They were to take a position of strong leadership. Paul says:

> "(We) *sent Timotheus, our brother, and minister of God, and our fellow-laborer in the gospel of Christ, to establish you, and to comfort you concerning your faith*" (I Thessalonians 3:2).

Ministers are to promote the Kingdom of God among men. Notice how Paul called Timothy a "fellow-laborer in the gospel of Christ." That is how ministers must look upon themselves, and one another, as co-laborers in the Lord's vineyards. They have an honorable office, yet it is one consisting of hard work. There should be no striving or contending over position or power. That hinders the work, not only of the gospel, but of each minister individually. Ministers should, if they are going to strive, strive together to carry on the great work in which they are engaged, to preach and publish the gospel of Christ and to persuade people to embrace and to live by it.

> *"For this reason I left you in Crete, that you would set in order what remains and appoint elders in every city as I directed you"* (Titus 1:5).

Paul had given instructions to Titus to ordain elders. These elders were ministers who were the older or mature, most understanding and experienced Christians. They were to have the authority, charge, and care of the churches. They were to feed and govern the people and to perform all pastoral work and duties toward the people. These were the fixed leaders. Those who labored in the Word and doctrine and were over the churches of the Lord. Paul had called for them to be appointed, but he had been in communication with the Lord and the Lord had shown him who to appoint. These elders were to dispense God's ordinances, to feed the Church of God over which the Holy Spirit had made them overseers because they were chosen for the perfecting of the saints and the edifying of the Body of Christ until we all come into unity of the faith unto a perfect man (Ephesians 4:12-13).

Notice, Paul told Titus "as I had appointed you." Everything must be ordered and maintained according to the direction of Christ and His chief ministers. Human traditions and inventions, such as electing ministers by the people, are recent adaptation of the Church. God appoints the offices as He pleases. In Titus chapter 1 the qualifications and character of the elder/bishops that Titus was to ordain are presented. Titus ordains through the direction of one (Paul) directed by God as to who was to be ordained and who was to be appointed. In 1 Peter 5:2, Peter calls on the elders or the pastors:

> *"Shepherd the flock of God among you, exercising oversight, not under compulsion, but voluntarily, according to the will of God; and not for sordid gain, but with eagerness."*

He calls upon them to preach the sincere Word of God and rule over the people according to the directions and disciplines the Word of God provides. He exhorts leaders to take the oversight, to watch over, and to be examples to the flock; but, he wants them to know that they cannot tyrannize or force the flock by compulsion, coercive force, or by imposing unscriptural or human conventions upon them. That is not their role. **The people are God's people**. They are not the pastor's people. They should be treated as God would treat them. Paul said in 2 Corinthians 1:24**:**

> *"Not that we lord it over your faith, but are workers with you for your joy; for in your faith you are standing firm."*

Jesus spoke of how the people should be treated in Matthew 20:25-27:

> *"But Jesus called them to Himself and said, "You know that the rulers of the Gentiles lord it over them, and their great men exercise authority over them. It is not this way among you, but whoever wishes to become great among you shall*

*be your servant, and whoever wishes to be first
among you shall be your slave."*

Thus we remember that the spiritual leader is **in**
authority and **under** authority. He is chosen by God. His
position is over God's people and not his own. **He should
treat them as Jesus would.** The ministers must labor among
their people, they are to rule in the Word (1 Timothy 5:17).
They must rule with love. They must not exercise dominion
as temporal lords, but rule as spiritual guides by setting a
good example to the flock. **Thus, they must rule the people
by Christ's laws and not their own.** We must trust the Lord
to direct our leaders. The leaders must instruct the people to
do well and reprove them when they do poorly. It is not
only their duty to give good counsel to the flock, but also to
give admonition and warning of dangers, to reprove for
negligence or other possible wrongs.

The founder, perfector and leader of the Church is
Christ. Christ called twelve disciples and they grew in
number to seventy (Luke 10:1), then many thousands. The
organization of the early church was not the same as in
many churches today. It was controlled by apostles, elders,
and other leaders. Christ knew He would be leaving, so He
trained and ordained ministers (Matthew 10, Luke 9, 10).
Christ commissioned leaders to follow His example in
everything (Matthew 28:18-20, Mark 16:15-20, Luke 24:48-52,
and Acts 1:4-8).

The early church had leaders. They were called apostles,
and eventually deacons, elders, prophets, evangelists,
pastors, and teachers (Ephesians 4:11, 1 Corinthians 12:28).
These church leaders had authority to make decisions that
affected the whole church. Officers were appointed in new
churches (Acts 14:23, Titus 1:5). They were given the care of

the churches. In instruction to the people (Hebrews 13:17) the writer said:

> *"Obey your leaders and submit to them, for they keep watch over your souls as those who will give an account. Let them do this with joy and not with grief, for this would be unprofitable for you."*

These leaders were called to watch over the souls of the people.

There were laws established for each of these endeavors. The early church was governed by predictable principles, no doubt, and according to cultural mores which we may never fully understand. The people were loyal to their leaders, as would be expected. Of course, in terms of the church, allegiance should be to God and not to a man (Acts 5:29). Its whole existence is for the purpose of glorifying God and evangelizing the world. The government of the Church is an absolute theocracy. That is, God reigning supreme in the life of each member, through Jesus Christ, by the power of the Holy Spirit, in accordance with the Word of God.

NEW TESTAMENT LEADERS

Authority, its usage and abuse is an important concept to understand. Much heartache could be avoided if we simply recognized God's view of authority. All authority begins and ends with Christ. God is sovereign over all, and He has given all authority to Christ for His church.

The church is governed by the Spirit. As such, and in light of the reality that all re-generated people have God's Spirit living within. The next level of authority is conscience. God made man with a free will, and intends for us to exercise our free will in obedience to His Word. Not even

God attempts to violate men and women in areas of personal choice not specifically governed in spiritual (you shalt not...). Man should not violate conscience either.

In the church, governance of authority is given to the five-fold ministry. Elders and deacons according to the measure of faith given by God. Of course, we should follow our leaders...as they follow Christ...and only then.

Most church leaders in the New Testament were ordained. Ordaining really means to choose, appoint, or set aside a person who is divinely called to a special ministry, in and for the Church. The person to be ordained should not be unless he is chosen by God, recognized by existing leaders, and set apart for that purpose. If not set apart directly by the Holy Spirit, then certainly by the leadership of the Church being led by the Spirit.

Ordination, of course, comes first and foremost from God. Jesus ordained. He ordained the twelve, then the seventy to represent Him. When He did, He gave them power (Matthew 10, Luke 1-8, 10:1-20, and Mark 6:7-13). He ordained the men that were chosen by the Holy Ghost and they were filled with faith and power to accomplish the tasks set before them. Leaders were chosen by God, then they were ordained by men (Acts 14:23, Titus 1:5).

The duties of those in leadership are many. Among them are:

- to perfect the saints (Ephesians 4:12)
- to watch over souls (Hebrews 13:17)
- to disciple other church leaders (2 Timothy 2:1-2)
- to preach (Titus 1:3)
- to exhort and rebuke (Titus 2:15)

Even though qualified by God, we are not sufficient in

ourselves to think anything of ourselves, but our sufficiency is of God.

> *"Not that we are adequate in ourselves to consider anything as coming from ourselves, but our adequacy is from God, who also made us adequate as servants of a new covenant, not of the letter but of the Spirit; for the letter kills, but the Spirit gives life"* (2 Corinthians 3:5-6).

This is the point where people cry out, "What is to protect us from anarchy, from a theocracy according to the pastor?" Theocracy is, in fact, God ruling, so if it is truly God ruling, then there is nothing to fear. There are several things that people can do.

First, the people must know the minister. As a shepherd knows the flock, so should the people know their shepherd. They must know his/her person, voice, acknowledging them as their spiritual leader paying due regard to his/her teachings, rulings, and admonitions. They must esteem their minister highly in love, they should value the office of the ministry, love and honor the persons of their ministry, and show their love and affection in proper ways. 1 Thessalonians 5:12-14 says:

> *"But we request of you, brethren, that you appreciate those who diligently labor among you, and have charge over you in the Lord and give you instruction, and that you esteem them very highly in love because of their work. Live in peace with one another. We urge you, brethren, admonish the unruly, encourage the fainthearted, help the weak, be patient with everyone."*

Thus, all can be done decently and in order. The people must also concern themselves with the fact that they are admonished in Hebrews 13:7,

> *"Remember those who led you, who spoke the
> word of God to you; and considering the result of
> their conduct, imitate their faith."*

Above all, the people should give true consideration to
Mark 11:22, where Jesus said, *"Have faith in God."* If God
placed a person in a ministry, (they should know whether
He did or not), then God also placed the leader in authority.
As a result of that, the people should continue to have faith
in God, knowing that God would not put them in a position
where they could be deceived or harmed. God is willing to
protect His people who are submitted to Him, even if the
one in authority is not wholly true to God. God can take His
people away from a leader who is in error. For God has said,

> *"Thus says the Lord GOD, "Behold, I am
> against the shepherds, and I will demand My
> sheep from them and make them cease from
> feeding sheep. So the shepherds will not feed
> themselves anymore, but I will deliver My flock
> from their mouth, so that they will not be food for
> them"'* (Ezekiel 34:10).

Until God delivers the people they are to have respect
for the authority.

Take the example of Samuel. Samuel was surrendered
by his mother, Hannah, to the priest, Eli, for his education
and instruction as a priest. However, Eli was not properly
fulfilling his rule and was told so by a man of God (1 Samuel
2:27-36). In fact, the Lord came to Samuel and shared with
him the fate of Eli (1 Samuel 3:11-14). But, Samuel had been
placed in Eli's care and God was honoring that commitment.
Samuel could not step into Eli's position because God had
yet to place him there. So, he quietly grew under Eli's

authority and care and the Lord was with him (1 Samuel 3:19-21).

David is another example of both trusting God and having respect for authority. God chose Saul to become King of Israel, but Saul had shown himself to be unfaithful to God so that God directed Samuel to anoint a new king. Samuel anointed David, still a child, to be king, and the Spirit of the Lord came upon David "from that day forward," and the Spirit of the Lord departed from Saul (1 Samuel 16:13-14). Although God had made His choice in the Spirit, Saul was still King of Israel and David would not be so until Saul was dead.

Although Saul sought to kill David, David was well aware of God's view of authority and waited for God. Saul did not have the anointing any longer, but he **had been** anointed. David was the true king, but God had not yet allowed him to fill that office. David showed all the proper respect for a person in authority, even if that person was wrong. He was content to see God dealing with the leadership. David once found himself in a position where he could have killed Saul, but he refused to do so.

> So he said to his men, "Far be it from me because of the LORD that I should do this thing to my lord, the LORD'S anointed, to stretch out my hand against him, since he is the LORD'S anointed" (1 Samuel 24:6).

In fact, in a conversation with Saul, David showed how much he trusted God. He never let his own desires or vision overrule God's timing. He simply told Saul,

> "May the LORD judge between you and me, and may the LORD avenge me on you; but my hand shall not be against you" (1 Samuel 24:12).

It was not David's season to be king. He knew he was to maintain his respect for the one in authority, until **God** told him otherwise. David had a second chance to kill Saul, but he was checked by an awareness of God's presence and he could not cross God's plans.

> "Then Abishai said to David, 'Today God has delivered your enemy into your hand; now therefore, please let me strike him with the spear to the ground with one stroke, and I will not strike him the second time.' But David said to Abishai, 'Do not destroy him, for who can stretch out his hand against the LORD'S anointed and be without guilt?' David also said, 'As the LORD lives, surely the LORD will strike him, or his day will come that he dies, or he will go down into battle and perish. The LORD forbid that I should stretch out my hand against the LORD'S anointed; but now please take the spear that is at his head and the jug of water, and let us go'" (1 Samuel 26:8-11).

David knew he would not be held guiltless should he come against an anointed one of God. He knew it was neither his nor the people's place to rehabilitate or remove authority, but it was God's, and God would do it in his own time. God has a purpose for all that He does. One does not always understand what that is at the time, but we know this: God is always correct and His judgment is exact and fair.

Of course, David did have the "anointing to duck and run" when King Saul tried to kill him with a spear. Further, when Paul was to be beaten and jailed he exercised his citizenship rights to avoid what would have been a truly bad day for him. We must be cautious, never give up our common sense, while giving every reasonable opportunity for a designated leader to lead with grace.

There is also another recourse that God provides in John 4:1-2:

> *"Beloved, believe not every spirit, but try the spirits whether they are of God: because many false prophets are gone out into the world. Hereby know ye the Spirit of God: Every spirit that confesseth that Jesus Christ is come in the flesh is of God."*

God wants people to "try the spirits," to know the truth. Knowing the truth is difficult at times, but by trying the spirits the people will come to know right from wrong. Ministers of the gospel should encourage people to ask questions where they are concerned.

Another action that can be taken is to rely on Proverbs 3:5-6:

> *"Trust in the LORD with all your heart, And do not lean on your own understanding. In all your ways acknowledge Him, And He will make your paths straight."*

If the path brought the people there, God knows where they are and God is going to take care of them. Jesus said:

> *"My sheep hear My voice, and I know them, and they follow Me"* (John 10:27).

> *"If I do not do the works of My Father, do not believe Me; but if I do them, though you do not believe Me, believe the works, so that you may*

know and understand that the Father is in Me,
and I in the Father" (John 10:37-38).

The people's responsibility in the congregation is to follow the one in charge. The people are to pray for their authority as Hebrews 13:7-17 and Romans 13 instruct them. They are to have respect, faith, and confidence in those above them in God's chain of command. **If they are not submitted to God, they can never submit to a leader of God**. They are to obey God's leader as long as they are not submitting to sin.

Men and women of God may require you to submit to situations which will cause your flesh to rebel, but we are not to judge what it does to our flesh. We are to submit to a leader's spirit if it lines up with God's Word.

Job 13:15 says, *"Though he slay me, yet will I trust in him."* Job had confidence and trust in God because he knew that God is fair and righteous in all that happened in this life. If one says he trusts God, he will trust the person whom God puts in charge. We are to trust God and His ability to work His will in, and through, the frailties of men. Murmurers and back-biters do not trust God.

As previously noted, a leader of God's responsibility is to watch men's souls, to watch over their development in a relationship with Jesus. If a teacher causes a student's relationship with Jesus to deteriorate by teaching error, then the teacher is held responsible by the Lord (Ezekiel 33:6, 8).

The devil sometimes uses people to come against the authority God has placed over them. We must be careful not to become more concerned about people than God (Matthew 6:24). One can never obey God if he looks at people's faces for assurance (Jeremiah 1:8, 17). A leader of God can only concern himself with obedience to God, knowing that God will only do the best for his people, whether they believe it or not. A leader can never let people get in the way of their responsibility to God. People pleasing has been the downfall of many. A leader compromises his position, as well as God's position, when he panders to the people.

RELATIONAL ROLES

All leaders will have various roles they must play, some enjoyable, some less so. These include shepherd, teacher, guide, healer, sustainer, comforter, administrator, and counselor. No one leader can do all of these equally well. Perhaps the one relational role most problematic for spiritual leaders is that of counselor, a role we briefly turn our attention too, along with the key responsibility of developing future leaders.

THE LEADER AS COUNSELOR

There are three broad levels of counsel used in Christian circles. These levels are determined by the type of need, and the qualifications of the counselor.

Ministry of the Word, personal application and direction of the Holy Spirit in revealing hidden issues of the heart should be a part of Holy Spirit-led counseling. This often requires sharing and uncovering the past, healing of memories, and a release from the barbs and chains of the enemy. This level of ministry is inadvisable without distinct leading from the Holy Spirit and training in counseling ministry.

Christian ethics will divert problems from developing. Clear lines of counsel can only be established as those given responsibility learn to be content and at peace, functioning within the realm of authority delegated to them. The two major sources of problems developing in this area are lack of definition in authoritative boundaries or competency, and personal insecurities and ambitions.

If someone comes to you and you are not a pastor (and, what is more, you are not familiar with the person and their problem) first realize you are in a potentially difficult situation. The burden of maintaining the unity of the Spirit, in relationship to the Body where you are, now rests with you. Your general goal is "to speak the same" so you must first find out what has been spoken before. You may ask the person these questions:

- "Have you spoken to the pastor or your regular counselor (or home group leader)?" This immediately lets them know of your loyalty and commitment to one another.

- "What did they say?" Be sure you don't counter-counsel or give advice different than what has been given.

- "Did you understand it clearly?" You may need to offer help to clarify the situation but do not offer fresh counsel. This is not an opportunity to subtly change their counsel, but to confirm and consolidate it. If you feel unwise counsel was given in the past, you should hold your peace until you can discuss things with the previous counselor.

     "For brothers to dwell together in unity...there the LORD commanded the blessing - life forever" (Psalm 133).

     "...that you all agree and that there be no divisions among you, but that you be made complete

in the same mind and in the same judgment" (1 Corinthians 1:10b).

DISCERN WHICH OF THE FOLLOWING CATEGORIES THE PERSON FALLS INTO:

Are they in direct disagreement and rebellion to the leadership?

Are they working one leader against another? Are they seeking some other counsel, or are they just not satisfied? Are they looking for someone to sympathize with them - someone who "understands them" Watch for subtle "sympathy-seekers." They often come on as humble and innocent or they may use the "weepy" approach, and elevate you or touch your ego and cause you to respond out of pride - "I didn't know who could help me, but then your name came into my mind."

Are they in genuine need of counsel? Even if they are in definite need of counsel, don't go in over your head or operate out of your realm. If it is a serious problem concerning mental or family areas, or a personal issue, you have no right to counsel privately unless you have a recognized ministry function and you have been equipped for those tasks within the body. You'll grow and learn by submitting to those whom God has put in the Body for that function. This best comes from being with a competent counselor, not from damaging lives and estranging yourself from your brethren by unknowingly becoming entangled or giving unwise advice. Flow as a team. Work as one body.

If you do counsel, let it be in areas you can handle safely, and then quickly relate it to those in leadership who are responsible for the person. There should be no secrets from pastor or elders except for confidential counseling, and even then only by previous agreement. They are the ones held accountable by God for the souls of the flock. You should state initially the limits to confidentiality.

Do not engage in counsel with those who indulge in railing against the church fellowship, or against the leadership (Proverbs 25:18-19). Beware the critical spirit. Do not agree with the person about their circumstances, but ask them to speak face to face with the one they are criticizing by saying, "Come with me, and we'll speak to the person now." The critic will either be speaking the truth, in which case the issue will get resolved, or else the gossip will be exposed and sin will be thwarted from continuing. Better a small crisis now than a shipwreck later on.

You should make it clear that what you say is not final, but that they are welcome to check your counsel with the pastor. This undermines using you for leverage and authority. You should disarm yourself before them of that type of authority, showing yourself submitted and loyal. Make it clear that direct counsel is not your final responsibility. The shepherd is the one God holds responsible.

Be sure of your own security and identity before you begin to counsel others. If you are not free from rejection, insecurity, false identity and fears, your endeavors at counseling will show some fruit (because God is faithful to his Word), but may result in hurting both the counselee and yourself! Because of **personal insecurity**, you will tend to be possessive of the counselee, and thus "lock them in" to you. This possessiveness leads to **domination and dependence**, causing the counselee to ultimately reject you. The consequence is both are hurt. Remember: our goal here is not to build up "our ministry" or "our church," but to be co-workers with God in the building of **His Church**.

CONFIDENCE AND TRUST

If you are caught gossiping or leaking information which you receive in counseling (either by boasting, or subtle inferences) you will destroy not only your personal credibility, but the one in the Body to whom you are joined. Beware of gossip in any form. Do not eavesdrop nor pry into other people's conversation when they are sharing problems. You will be told what you need to know. Always retain confidence both with your counselee and the senior leader to whom God has given charge of the flock.

Never counsel a person of the opposite sex without: a) either two brothers, or b) a husband and wife team, or c) a person of the same sex present. Give no grounds to the enemy for false accusations.[16]

Paul urged the Church in Corinth to counsel or give comfort in the areas where they had been comforted or counseled by God In other words, in the areas where the grace and power of God had established freedom one was free to minister God's grace (2 Corinthians 1:3-7). We have an obligation to provide helpful and effective counsel in our leadership positions for the benefit of the church.

THE DEVELOPMENT OF A LEADER

One of the most important responsibilities a leader has is finding potential leaders and training them for church or business leadership.

Only leaders can reproduce leaders. Leaders are not born but grown (developed). Some people are born with

---

[16] For more information/training on counseling skills, see Dr. DeKoven's book, *On Belay: An Introduction to Christian Counseling.*

special strengths and abilities that add to their leadership abilities, but ultimately leaders are to be developed.

I've never seen an effective leader who, at some time or other, did not have another leader as his/her mentor. That is the advantage of sitting under and working with a well-developed ministry. It puts you light years ahead of others, preparing you for the time when you begin to minister on your own.

Great leaders don't develop themselves. Non-leaders can't reproduce a leader, because much of what is taught is through visual example. It's impossible to just teach by theory.

So, as leaders, we do the best we can to develop our leadership skills and be all we can be, because we will produce what we are.

There is a Three-Step Process in developing and growing leaders:

First, we must discern. We have to know who our potential leaders are. It takes one to know one...usually.

Second, once we select those to mentor, we must demonstrate. After we find the person with potential, we have to model leadership for them. It takes one to show one.

Third, we must develop a leader. We have to grow them. It takes one to grow one.

Let's look at these three primary steps to leader development in greater depth.

Discernment - How do I discern leadership abilities in others? Well, it takes one to know one. That is, with God's help we draw to ourselves what we are. We will discern the same potential as our own. In that sense, like attracts like. As the Lord brings people into the church, some will have similar characteristics to our own. Of course, we must be careful in that our negative and positive characteristics attract equally. Thus, we must be open to the Holy Spirit's direction.

As we follow the Holy Spirit, we will find under shepherds with the following characteristics.

They are willing and faithful (2 Timothy 2:2). This should go without saying. However, many leaders will be attracted by the packaging and not the tested product. I will take faithfulness and character over charming anytime. (Both are best!)

Further, they will influence others for the kingdom. They will influence their families, peers, other families, peer groups, even other leaders. One cannot help but notice someone with wisdom before their time or knowledge above what is expected (Luke 2:45-47).

Leaders will submit their ideas to others, with a confidence that their ideas should be implemented. They are willing to ask questions, they are not just YES men.

Leaders will be driven by their vision. Potential leaders help others to talk about their vision and begin to lay claim to part of it. They are equally interested in seeing the vision come to pass.

Also, leaders should relate well to people. Skills are important, as is gifting, but a potential leader must be a people person to succeed.

Leaders should be able to handle pressure. The value of

a leader is known by what he can do and what he can take in terms of the pressure of leadership. A person that runs from conflict (e.g., Jonah) cannot function well in leadership.

Leaders should have the ability to solve problems effectively, and not be afraid to tackle a difficult project, nor do they avoid a challenge. Further, potential leaders will be effective communicators. Their verbal and written skills are developed sufficiently to ensure clarity of thought and direction.

A potential leader must have confidence in the Lord and himself; and will have a positive, forward look toward the church and ministry.

Finally, a potential leader wants to be evaluated by his results, and respected for his production not his position.

You may not find a person who fits all of this description. That should not discourage you. The thing is to find one with some of the desired characteristics and concentrate on developing the others over time.

As a leader with charges who are younger in the Lord, the following advice is requisite:

DEMONSTRATE -IT TAKES ONE TO SHOW ONE.

As leaders, we have a two-fold responsibility. We need to lead so others will follow, by modeling good leadership. Our lifestyle, work habits, and attitudes will be picked up by those around us. Thus we must ensure that we are living properly before the Lord, for like begets like.

DEVELOP -IT TAKES ONE TO GROW ONE.

It takes time to develop a leader. It took approximately 3 years before the first deacons were developed in Jerusalem.

It will take time to mature a leader. Thus, we must choose future leaders with the utmost care.

Your choice will determine your success. When searching for leaders, choose people who portray a great desire (with potential) to succeed, yet remember that no one (including and especially yourself) is perfect. Challenge them to stretch in their relationship with the Lord by taking responsibility in the Church.

Once you have begun a "Timothy" relationship, you must be willing to bring them into your inner circle, teach them what you know and allow them to experience you as a person and leader. Vulnerability is needed, but is to be shared slowly. Familiarity too quickly leads to contempt.

Finally, you must be willing to supervise and lovingly correct your disciple from the Word, not to discourage, but to encourage greater depth in their relationships and in their leadership capability.

CONCLUSION

The call of God to lead in the Church is an awesome one. The burden of leadership, especially in urban centers, can create an overwhelming pressure. Even the best of God's men and women can border on burnout unless balance, support and spiritual vitality can be maintained in the leader's life.

Leaders need vision and ability to develop an objective plan which is Holy Spirit inspired. Vision and charisma are not sufficient to ensure success in ministry. All of our work as shepherds and leaders should flow from a heart of compassion, a heart transformed by God's power. We are to live a life of faith, yet faith works by love. Without the love of God compelling us we will not fulfill our destiny in God no matter how large our "work" might become.

The Lord's call is a call to servanthood, mutual accountability, and commitment. The principles of sowing and reaping can be seen in the leader-to-sheep relationship. Unfortunately, for many outstanding men and women of God, they reap what <u>other</u> leaders have sown. In spite of this, we are all responsible to sow life so that other leaders who might inherit our sheep will have a solid foundation upon which to build.

Every leader desires to be all God has intended them to be. As God's favor continues to flow in a leader's life, and as we apply principles of careful management along with good ethics, we will see success in the labor of our hands.

APPENDIX 1

QUALIFICATIONS FOR ELDERS IN THE

NEW TESTAMENT CHURCH

Because of the important leadership role elders must play, God has given certain personal qualifications. Kevin J. Conner, in his book, *The Church in the New Testament* (Blackburn, Victoria, Australia: Conner Publications, 1987, pp. 110-117), has categorized the qualifications of eldership as follows:

SPIRITUAL QUALIFICATIONS

- Born again

- Water baptized

- Baptized and filled with the Holy Spirit

- Called by the Holy Spirit, recognized by the people

CHARACTER QUALIFICATIONS

- Blameless
- Of good behavior
- Vigilant
- Temperate
- Sober

- Just

- Holy

- Lover of good

- Hospitable

- Patient

- Not a brawler

- Not easily angered

- Not a striker

- Not greedy

- Not covetous

- Not self-willed

- Not given to wine

- Of good report

- Grave (Honorable)

- Not double-tongued

- Not a slanderer

- Faithful in all things

- Steward of God

- Must desire office

- Not a lord over God's people

- An example to the people of God

DOMESTIC QUALIFICATIONS

- Able to rule his own house well
- Husband of one wife
- Wife must be grave
- Wife must not be slanderous
- Wife must be sober
- Wife must be faithful in all things
- Children in subjection
- Children have gravity
- Children faithful
- Children not accused of riot
- Children not unruly

MINISTRY QUALIFICATIONS

- Called by the Holy Spirit
- Hold fast the faithful Word as he has been taught
- Able to teach
- Able to exhort and convince
- Not a novice
- Able to shepherd the flock of God

APPENDIX 2

DESCRIPTIONS OF THE FIVE-FOLD MINISTRY

Apostle (*apostolos* = one sent with a commission). This person is charged with extending the Church and providing government and structure. He works in areas the other ministry gifts work in as he establishes churches. First, he ministers as an evangelist to gain converts for the new church. Then, he teaches them the truths of the gospel so that they will grow in the faith. He pastors them for a time as the church is stabilized, all the while operating in gifts of prophecy as needed. The apostle trains and appoints new leaders of the Church and goes on to begin other works. Thereafter he retains apostolic oversight of the Church and pastors.

Prophets (*prophetes* = one who foretells). This person is a special messenger of God with special abilities to see into the future, see the spiritual realm, and hear the voice in ways others cannot hear. Many times he prophesies to church leaders, governmental leaders, and others in places of influence and government. He is God's voice in the affairs of the earth.

Evangelist (*euanggelistes* = one who tells good news). This person is charged with the task of proclaiming the good news. To the lost this means salvation. To the children of the kingdom it means deliverance.

Pastor (*poiomen* = shepherd). This person has charge of the local flock to care for, nurture, protect, and feed. His ministry is close to home and directly related to the people he serves over a long period of time.

Teacher (*didoskolos* = instructor). This person explains the Scriptures in ways the other ministry gifts cannot. He is able to make the Word of God plain in the minds of the people, and make specific application to everyday life.

Bibliography

Cann, Gilbert. *Liberating Leadership*, TLC Publishers, Australia, 1989

Covey, S.R. *The 7 Habits of Highly Effective People*, Fireside Books. Simon & Shuster: New York, 1990

Damazio, Frank. *Making of a Leader.* Bible Temple Publishing

DeKoven, Stan, *On Belay: Introduction to Christian Counseling*, Vision Publishing, Ramona, CA

IBID, *Pastoral Leadership: In the Eye of the Storm*, Vision Publishing, Ramona, CA

IBID, *Supernatural Architecture: Preparing the Church of the 21st Century*, Wagner Publishing, Colorado Springs, Co. 2003

Gangel, Kenneth O. *Feeding & Leading.* Scribner Publishing.

Moulton, H. ed, *The Analytical Greek Lexicon.* (Revised). Grand Rapids: Zondervan Publishing. 1977

Nanus, Burt. *Visionary Leadership.* Jossey-Bass, 1990

Peter, J.T. & Woferman, Jr., R.H. *In Search of Excellence.* Harper & Row: New York, NY. 1982

Placque, Walmart Stores

Anderson, Leith, *Leadership that Works,* Bethany House Publishing, 2002

Blanchard, Kenneth, *Leadership Smarts,* Honor Books, 2004

IBID, with Hybels, Bill and Hodges, Phil, *Leadership by the Book,* Waterbrook Publishing, 1999

Maxwell, John, *The 21 Irrefutable laws of Leadership,* Nelson/Word Publishing Group, 1998

Phillips, Donald, *Lincoln on Leadership*, Warner Books, 1993

Ford, Leighton, Transforming Leadership, Intervarsity Press, 1993

OTHER BOOKS BY THE AUTHOR

- Addiction Counseling

- Christian Education

- Crisis Counseling

- Family Violence: Patterns of Destruction

- 40 Days to the Promise

- Fresh Manna: How to Study the Word

- From a Father's Heart

- Grief Relief

- Healing Community: Developing A Counseling Ministry

- Homiletics

- I Want To Be Like you Dad: Breaking Generational Patterns Restoring the Father's Heart

- Journey Through the New Testament

- Journey Through the Old Testament

- Journey to Wholeness

- Keys to Successful Living

- Living Fruitfully

- Marriage & Family Life

- New Apostolic Schools

- New Beginnings

- On Belay!

- Parenting on Purpose

- Pastoral Ministry

- Research Writing Made Easy

- Strategic Church Administration

- Supernatural Architecture

- That's the Kingdom of God

- Transferring the Vision

- 12 Steps to Wholeness